In the Middle of Nowhere

J.M. Coetzee in South Africa

Jonathan Crewe

University Press of America,® Inc.
Lanham • Boulder • New York • Toronto • Plymouth, UK

Copyright © 2016 by University Press of America,® Inc.
4501 Forbes Boulevard, Suite 200, Lanham, Maryland 20706
UPA Acquisitions Department (301) 459-3366

Unit A, Whitacre Mews, 26-34 Stannary Street,
London SE11 4AB, United Kingdom

All rights reserved
Printed in the United States of America
British Library Cataloguing in Publication Information Available

Library of Congress Control Number: 2015952708
ISBN: 978-0-7618-6693-0 (pbk : alk. paper)—ISBN: 978-0-7618-6694-7 (electronic)

Cover Art: William Kentridge, Lekkerbreek, 2013. Courtesy of David Krut Publishing.

Excerpts from "X" and "XI" from THE HEIGHTS OF MACCHU PICCHU by Pablo Neruda, translated by Nathaniel Tarn. Translation copyright © 1966, renewed © 1994 by Nathaniel Tarn. Reprinted by permission of Farrar, Straus and Giroux, LLC.

"Gnosticism IV" from DECREATION: POETRY, ESSAYS, OPERA by Anne Carson, copyright © 2005 by Anne Carson. Used by permission of Alfred A. Knopf, an imprint of the Knopf Doubleday Publishing Group, a division of Penguin Random House LLC. All rights reserved.

∞™ The paper used in this publication meets the minimum requirements of American National Standard for Information Sciences Permanence of Paper for Printed Library Materials, ANSI/NISO Z39.48-1992.

Contents

	Acknowledgments	v
	Introduction	1
1	Arrival	17
2	Settling In	31
3	Flashbacks	49
4	Boyhood	69
5	*Disgrace*	89
6	Master Classes: *White Writing*	105

Acknowledgments

My principal debts are not to institutions but to individuals who read all or parts of the manuscript at various stages and contributed many valuable suggestions. These readers include David Attwell, Rita Barnard, Jessica Crewe, Lars Engle, Stephen Orgel, James Shapiro, Peter Swaab, and, above all, my partner, Melissa Zeiger. I am grateful as well for support from my colleagues in the humanities at Dartmouth, and for research funding attached to the Leon Black Chair of Shakespearean Studies at Dartmouth, which I occupied until June, 2015. My deepest, incalculable, personal debts are owed, first, to my beloved partner Melissa Zeiger, to whom I dedicate this book, and to my daughter Jessica, for personal and professional support.

I wish to thank *English in Africa* for permission to include in this book a revised version of "Arrival: J.M. Coetzee in Cape Town," *EIA*, 40, 1 (May, 2013), 11-36.

Introduction

I have borrowed the phrase that gives this book its title from the monologue of J.M. Coetzee's tragicomic protagonist Magda in the novel *In the Heart of the Country,* who feels as if she is "in the middle of nowhere."[1] Magda is one of Coetzee's series of subjectively invested protagonists or fictional avatars. An aging, poignant, disconcerting, consciously crazy spinster, living in isolation on a remote sheep farm in the South African Karroo, she is represented as being subject, to an unusual degree, to the gift and curse of language: "Am I a monologue moving through time, approximately five feet above the ground, if the ground does not turn out to be just another word, in which case I am lost indeed"(62). As a drastically isolated consciousness in a barren, unappealing woman's body, denied meaningful sociocultural location and connection, Magda epitomizes in the first instance a predicament of the colonial woman from Olive Schreiner through Doris Lessing to Nadine Gordimer. Unlike the silent, insentient colonial patriarch or empire-builder, she is hyper-sentient, but at the cost of her sanity.[2]

The "mad" female protagonist of Coetzee's aggressively postmodern, feminist-inflected novel belongs partly to a post-nineteenth century fictional world in which the isolated, housebound woman, wife or single daughter, has become the locus of white colonial consciousness. Her situation is not unambiguous: Coetzee's abjected spinster Magda, who, like her author, channels literary and intellectual history, is an extraordinarily emancipated and even ribald commentator on her world, yet once the irony has been savored, the crippling psychic and social facts of her condition remain. Such is the old/new woman's story of an African farm.[3]

Insofar as Coetzee projects Magda as one of his fictional avatars, she articulates in drastic fashion his own sense of being in the middle of nowhere in South Africa. A more tempered articulation characterizes his quasi-autobiographical writings, *Boyhood, Youth*, and *Summertime*, collected as a trilogy under the title *Scenes from Provincial Life*, in which he becomes his fictional persona, John.[4] The borderline in Coetzee's work between autobiography and fiction is tenuous—i.e. formal—at best, however, since Coetzee avatars, sometimes so named, populate much of his fiction, their gender being partly a function of differing sensibilities and imagined social positions. Coetzee's trilogy recharacterizes Magda's "nowhere" (with a nod to Flaubert) as the provinces. These provinces are not wholly synonymous with nowhere, but they are a phenomenon of colonial and/or post-colonial marginality. Not without a complex history, the South African provinces are a site of white colonial privilege, yet by the same token of colonial shame, mortification, and removal from urbane metropolitan culture, seemingly devoid of any "higher" significance. This provincial condition, troped as being in the middle of nowhere, may seem like a distinctively white, colonial one, unlike that of the indigenous peoples with their own languages, cultures, and complex history, and possibly with a greater sense of African identity than whites like Magda. Of all this cultural and historical diversity, the subjects of Coetzee's "provincial" renderings seem largely oblivious. It seems clear from fiction written by writers of color, however, that not only whites experience the provincial condition as such; it is a condition potentially or actually internalized by many colonial subjects of the erstwhile British imperium.

One feature of Coetzee's work is the exploration of how the threadbare texture and often-embarrassing peculiarities of the provinces can be made to *signify* in a literary sphere that has become increasingly global in his lifetime. Such is Magda's defeated ambition, but she also has the sense that being in the middle of nowhere offers opportunities for exhilarating self-invention or even world-invention. She oscillates wildly between a sense of non-being and divine being as the creator of a world emanating from her consciousness, one that will cease with her death. From her perspective, nowhere and everywhere are not necessarily distinct, and being "nowhere" can signify an existential condition in the world—even a metaphysical abyss—to which Coetzee's often "placeless" fictions continue to attest. No doubt Magda figures an unmoored extremism ultimately inimical to the vocation of the novelist. She says as much when she observes that her vocation is for first-person lyric rather than narrative; that vocation culminates in her effort to compose in a pseudo-Spanish "language of pure meanings" (125), written in white stones—stretching the point, her *rime petrose*—and addressed to aliens flying above the earth. Being without a human audience also means, however, astringently rejecting a "native" tradition, both English and Afrikaans, of plangent, sentimental lyricism, as Magda does right at the end of the book:

> There are poems, I am sure, about the heart that aches for the Verlore Vlakte, about the melancholy of the sunset over the koppies, the sheep beginning to

huddle against the first evening chill, the faraway boom of the windmill, the first chirrup of the first cricket, the last twitterings of the birds in the thorn trees, the stones of the farmhouse still holding the sun's warmth, the kitchen lamp glowing steady. They are poems I could write myself . . . but I thought it was too easy (138).

Betraying just a trace of satanic pride, Magda prefers the "impossible" task of soliciting aliens to the easier one of becoming a "South African poet."

If there are important ways in which Magda is a stand-in for Coetzee, his ambition—in which he has succeeded by any reckoning—was to escape Magda's predicament, in other words, not merely to be a writer without audience marooned in the middle of nowhere. That also meant not being a "provincial" writer; he is now, in fact, the Nobel-prizewinning global author par excellence. Leaving the provinces behind in every sense was obviously one condition of this breakout into global significance, yet both Coetzee's autobiographies and his fiction attest to the impossibility of getting the provinces out of his system, or of attaining any fictionalized self-understanding that does not begin with them, in the middle of nowhere. It is partly my own sense of beginning in the middle of the same nowhere that has drawn me to his fiction and autobiography; extended reading of Coetzee as well as the personal encounters recalled in this book have only reinforced my sense of affinity.

In my first chapter, I describe how I was unexpectedly prompted to write the book. The book attests to my forty-year friendship with Coetzee, periodically renewed, yet most crucially to my first encounter with him in the years 1972–74, when we happened to arrive simultaneously as English lecturers in the University of Cape Town. I begin with recollections of those years before moving on both to some later vignettes and to commentary on *Boyhood* and *Disgrace*, the latter capable of being read as Coetzee's South African "goodbye to all that," that aspire to be both informed and informing. I do not remotely claim to capture Coetzee's singularity as a writer, nor do I suggest that South Africa supplies the "key" to his meanings. Quite the contrary, since Coetzee has never identified himself as a "South African writer." My book is accordingly a hybrid, comprising both recollection and critical commentary. If it belongs to a genre, perhaps it is that of "personal criticism" as a methodological outgrowth of feminist criticism, but here without the feminist polemics that launched the genre in the 1990s.[5] The book belongs, that is to say, to the genre that legitimizes memoir, testimony, and personally inflected criticism alongside, or in place of, impersonal academic commentary. The circumstances that dictated this generic choice will become apparent in what follows.

Assuming a high level of interest in Coetzee on the part of both general and academic readers, the book is addressed to both those constituencies, as well as to readers inside and outside South Africa. I begin, as I said, with the years 1972–74 during which Coetzee and I met and overlapped in the English Department of the University of Cape Town. Those two years were momentous ones for both of us. For me they entailed a move from the even more provincial province of Natal (now Kwazulu-Natal) to Cape Town, while for Coetzee they were years of return to South Africa after a decade abroad. Coetzee had just returned from the United States, where he had been teaching at SUNY Buffalo after having completed his Ph.D. at the University of Texas, Austin. Returning to the Cape Town University English Department must surely have seemed like a come-down to him after having taught at Buffalo in the golden age of Leslie Fiedler and cutting-edge theory. (I would learn in due course what had precipitated his return.) Nevertheless, it was in these years, politically somber as they were in South Africa, that Coetzee's career as a major novelist also took flight, with the publication of *Dusklands*.[6] Clearly both Cape Town and South Africa proved enabling as well as trying for him. Coetzee's focus on precisely the years 1972–74 in his "posthumous" fictionalized memoir, *Summertime: A Fiction* (2009), implicitly attests to their importance to him.

Coetzee initially struck me as mysterious. That was partly because, at that time, the American track into the South African academy was nothing like as well beaten as it is now, and academic norms and manners, especially in English Departments, were still British. This was really my first encounter with a South African colleague made in America. Coetzee also came from a different intellectual planet from that of all English-speaking South African writers and academics of my acquaintance. He was bringing with him an intellectual itinerary and formation far more widely recognized in the world outside than in South Africa at that time, e.g. in Buffalo. What Coetzee brought with him was, in short, both postmodernism and a theoretical sophistication corresponding to it. Formal training in linguistics as well as knowledge of European languages equipped him technically for stylistic analysis and also informed his own self-reflexive practice as a writer. Many South African readers, accustomed to English novelistic realism, found the Coetzee phenomenon baffling and even obnoxious, although others were quick to seize on its innovative promise. What could not be apparent at once, although it became so within the decade, was that the Coetzee "agenda" entailed little less than the undoing and reconfiguration of the colonial category "South African Literature." His critical book *White Writing* crossed linguistic boundaries between English and Afrikaans as well as generic ones between literary and non-literary writing.[7] Although it would take time for Coetzee to become a global writer, that potential, and, indeed, that ambition, were inherent in his work from the start. Both those features of Coetzee's work have been contentious, mainly in South Africa but also beyond its borders. I shall return to this topic in due course, but suffice to say here that both the scale of

Coetzee's ambition and his successful breakout into world literature have, on one hand, inspired admiration barely this side idolatry, and, on the other hand, a certain grudging, nativist resentment. (That split has characterized the reception of a number of postcolonial writers like Rushdie with a global readership.)

The world of canonized "South African Literature" Coetzee entered as a self-made alien generally meant poetry and fiction that constituted a respectable, colonial subset of canonical "English Literature." Usual suspects included Olive Schreiner, Pauline Smith, Alan Paton, the young Nadine Gordimer, Dan Jacobson, Roy Campbell, Guy Butler, Sidney Clouts, Douglas Livingstone, and the insurgent Athol Fugard. Writers of color like Es'kia Mphahlele (*Down Second Avenue*, 1959) and Alex la Guma (*A Walk in the Night*, 1962) hovered between South African Literature and African Literature. Sol Plaatje's now widely admired *Mhudi* (pub. 1930), seldom featured as more than a curiosity when it was remembered at all. "Afrikaans Literature" belonged to a separate category, partly because "South African Literature" was generally taken to mean works written in English and partly because many writers in Afrikaans were dedicated political and cultural nationalists. One colonial paradox of South African English Departments was that they scarcely gave the time of day to South African Literature, hewing closely instead to English Literature in its most elevated canonical guise.

Some of the preconditions and consequences of Coetzee's "arrival" in Cape Town—both literal arrival and arrival as a global novelist in the making—will be outlined, insofar as I understand them, in the pages that follow. Coetzee's work is now of course the subject of a major critical industry, featuring extensively in the critical research of currently graduating Ph.D.s in modern literature. I have taken account of some of the major critical work in this book, but production continues beyond my ability to keep pace (if anything, overproduction now, from which effects of fatigue and backlash can be expected to follow). In what follows, I write as Coetzee's contemporary and early reader more than as a specialist, playing, to the extent I can, the role of native informant to his global readership and of both native and emigrant commentator on his work.

Although I include personal recollection, I do not undertake formal biography. The late J.C. Kannemeyer performed that task in his heavily researched *J.M. Coetzee: A Life in Writing*.[8] If the canonizing monumentality of the book has elicited some adverse comment, it is currently the indispensable first resort for those seeking biographical information about Coetzee.[9] Here, I have tried not to retail what is now essentially common knowledge or gossip about Coetzee in Cape Town and abroad, and I have also tried to avoid redundant duplication of information available in the Kannemeyer biography. Occasionally, I have cross-referenced Kannemeyer in my own account, but have not felt obliged to do so continuously. To the extent that I rely on personal recollection and letters, thereby intruding upon the domain of the memoirist, I am also highly conscious of the biographical bind Coetzee anticipates in *Summertime*. Responding to a fictional literary biographer of the late J.M. Coetzee, the fictional interviewee Julia says:

> Mr. Vincent, I am perfectly aware it is John you want to hear about, not me. But the only story involving John that I can tell, or the only one I am prepared to tell, is this one, namely the story of my life and his part in it, which is quite different, quite another matter from, the story of his life and my part in it (43).

In a sense, this too is "the only story I can tell." If that means wishing to represent or lay claim to "my Coetzee"—to borrow a phrase from Hedley Twidle[10] —I am also conscious that no proprietary bid in the domain of Coetzee criticism and biography can have the slightest prospect of success. I have included autobiographical elements that some readers may find gratuitous and self-advertising, yet they are intended to fill in a picture of the world from which white, South African contemporaries of a certain generation, now both living abroad, emerged. It is a vanished world that will, in many ways, strike readers as bizarre, but, as Coetzee's autobiographies imply, it is also one in that curiously persists both personally and culturally. In addition to producing recollections, I blend in Coetzee's works of fictionalized autobiography. That principally means the autobiographical trilogy, but I have also included *Disgrace*, partly on the principle that its protagonist, too, is a Coetzee avatar. I do not consider Coetzee's writings after *Disgrace* (1999) because that is the point at which my capacity to inform sharply diminishes. That was the moment of Coetzee's emigration to Australia: whether that relocation was what Magda calls a move "from nowhere to nowhere, without beginning or end" (63), I cannot say. I am not unaware of the global impact of Coetzee's writings about animals in particular, or of the "new" ethics and politics those writings connote,[11] yet after *Disgrace* his new fictional avatar, Elizabeth Costello, came to the fore, signifying for me that Coetzee had become, in a strong sense, "other" than his former self. An Australian colleague, Andrew McCann, tells me that Coetzee's works written in Australia show generic and topical features of Australian writing (and Patrick White has always been a presence in Coetzee's work), but if so, those traits are unknown to me.

Although I have credited Coetzee with the undoing of "South African Literature," it is nevertheless his works written in a South African frame that remain most resonant, intelligible, and highly charged to me, and they are also the ones to which I feel I have a certain "native" access. In fact, to lay my cards on the table, it is those books, particularly *Dusklands, In the Heart of the Country, Waiting for the Barbarians*, and *Disgrace*, that constitute, for me, Coetzee's most powerful and moving achievement. I have read all Coetzee's books with differing degrees of interest and admiration, but the books I have named stand out for me as the deeply distinctive, incandescent ones, in which Coetzee raised the level of what it meant to write ("write" being the operative word) in and from Southern Africa, and in relation to its intense cultural pressures. It follows that I cannot do justice to what J.C. Kannemeyer and others have called (with whatever degree of irony given Coetzee's recourse to "posthumous" fiction) the "late" Coetzee.

Politically, the book spans the landmark transition in South Africa from the era of apartheid to that of post-apartheid. Coetzee's *Disgrace*, the subject of my final chapter, registers that long-awaited yet complex and problematic transition, which some would now characterize as a transition from racist colony to dysfunctional post-colony. Both our lives began early in World War II, in 1940 and 1941 respectively. Both Coetzee and I were born into families in which fathers were absent, having volunteered for service in the South African army, fighting on the side of the allies in North Africa and Europe. Mothers accordingly loomed large in our psychic and material lives. Both of us spent our childhood and adolescence in postwar South Africa under the ever-lengthening shadow of apartheid, enforced through militantly racist legislation and police action by the Afrikaner Nationalist government of D.F. Malan and his successors, which came to power in 1948. Many members of the Nationalist Party had sided with the Nazis, and had been interned for the duration of the war.

If, from the outside, black-white racial division looks like the defining one of apartheid politics, it was not necessarily that division that seemed most salient to young whites growing up in South Africa. In a sense, the whole point of apartheid was to render black people and their politics invisible to whites. If asked to state the population of South Africa, whites would not uncommonly say three million, the number of the white population only at that time. The correct answer would have been closer to fifteen million. The erasure of blacks from white consciousness meant that as children whites might well be more aware of antipathy between whites of English and Afrikaner descent or affiliation, with the Boer War in the historical background, than of conflict between whites and blacks. Obliviousness of black cultural and political history, including that of the ANC with its emergent leader, Nelson Mandela, could be virtually complete, especially outside the industrialized region around Johannesburg. The counterpart to this obliviousness was ignorance of any black language.

Such was the "boyhood" condition to which this book no less than Coetzee's *Boyhood* attests. In my case, English-Afrikaner antipathy played out at school in street fights and intensified sporting rivalries across the divide. Politically, that juvenile antipathy echoed to some degree the party conflict between the United Party (U.P.) and the militant, successful Nationalist Party ("Nats"), which had came to power in 1948. A strong residue of Afrikaner bitterness at the deaths of many Afrikaner women and children in English concentration camps infused—and was exploited in—Afrikaner Nationalist politics.[12] Among English speakers, antipathy to the "Nats" included a strong anti-Afrikaner prejudice. That polarization carried over to, but was also reconfigured to some degree at, the university level: on one hand, many English youth underwent some political consciousness-raising in the liberal English language universities, while, on the other, most Afrikaner youth became hardened in the academic citadels of white, Afrikaner nationalism.

The postwar polarization between Afrikaans and English speakers, fomented by the Nationalist Government, nevertheless belied a significant bilingual and bicultural history among whites, especially in the Cape Province of Coetzee's boyhood. The Afrikaner J.C. Smuts, wartime leader of the United Party, had been a Boer War general who had gone on to be educated in England at Cambridge, where he distinguished himself. It was a virtual axiom that the U.P. had to be led by an Afrikaner to have any hope of electoral victory, since Afrikaners were the white majority.

It was to the more easy-going bilingual "Cape" world that the Coetzee family belonged despite its Dutch-Afrikaner heritage. As Coetzee recalls in *Boyhood*:

> Greedily he drinks in the atmosphere, drinks in the happy, slapdash mixture of English and Afrikaans that is their common tongue when they get together. He likes this funny, dancing language, with its particles that slip here and there in the sentence. It is lighter, airier than the Afrikaans they study at school, which is weighed down with idioms that are supposed to come from the *volksmond*, the people's mouth, but seem to come only from the Great Trek, lumpish, nonsensical idioms about wagons and cattle and cattle-harness (81).

Until 1951, the Cape political world had also included "colored"—i.e., mixed race—people, most of whom were Afrikaans native speakers. Although disadvantaged, these people were included in the common voting roll and participated along with whites in general elections until their disenfranchisement under the Separate Registration of Voters Act in 1951. The "old" Cape world, formerly a British colony, was very much the setting of Coetzee's boyhood and an abiding presence in his fictional consciousness. It remained sheltered to a degree from the violent intransigence of the former Boer Republics and a world apart from "English" Natal in which the British imperial vision and the legacy of the "Zulu Wars" died hard.

In *Boyhood*, the narrating protagonist records his perception of black people, as distinct from the autochthonous "Hottentots," as aliens in the Western Cape. That perception does, of course, have a historical basis, since the main regions of early black settlement were the South African east coast and adjacent interior, yet the actual treatment of black people as non-indigenous aliens was by no means confined to the Western Cape; it increasingly became a fundamental tenet of "separate development." While the boy-narrator is explicitly critical of the treatment of black people, and thinks they are better than their oppressive "brothers" in the racial parable he recites, the adult John in *Summertime* reiterates, almost by way of apology, his cognitive, affective, and linguistic distance from black people. (The narrator in *Summertime* acknowledges that he knows none of the black languages, the typical situation of whites of our generation, when no black languages were taught in white schools.) That distance may help to account for a feature of Coetzee's writing that has repeatedly drawn comment, namely, his seeming inability or unwillingness to represent the subjectivity of black characters, or, in effect, to "identify" with them.

Clearly, such characterizations cannot be produced to order, and neither good intentions nor political sympathies—i.e., setting aside ill-intentioned caricatures or coarse ideological stereotypes—suffice to produce a compelling representation. Nor, of course, does the uncritical representation of persons of color who can merely be said to have internalized the discourse of the master. Indeed, my postscript on *White Writing* suggests that the white writer in South Africa is subject to a double bind from which there is no easy escape. On one hand, the virtual absence of black characters (or people) in white writing (notably the *plaasroman*) becomes a hugely conspicuous omission, whereas, on the other hand, representations of people of color by writers like Mikro and Alan Paton, especially when those characters speak in dialect or other languages, betray their authors. In other words, they say more about the readership of that fiction or about the interpretation the authors wish to impose than about the persons represented. There is good reason, in other words, for white writers to look before they leap into representing persons of color, marked as such, a rule I believe Coetzee has observed.[13] Nevertheless, a sense of disappointment or even hurt (to go no further than that) persists: at a dinner I attended after the publication of *Disgrace*, several prominent black writers attested to the sense of hurt even while affirming their respect for Coetzee as a writer.

My own heritage, as distinct from Coetzee's, was "English"—or Anglo-Jewish—although my early years were spent on a farm in the northeastern corner of the country—in the middle of nowhere indeed—where Afrikaners formed the white majority. Afrikaans was the primary medium of exchange between whites and blacks. I therefore started off bilingual, or strictly, trilingual, with some fluency in the black Sesotho language (a linguistic endowment that didn't survive my parents' moves to other parts of the country). Encountering Coetzee in life and in fiction meant encountering an exact contemporary with whom I shared a great deal that belonged to growing up white in the South Africa of our youth, so much so that when *Boyhood* was published my response was "well, at least I don't have to write an autobiography now," yet there were differences to be processed, arising from our not fully shared familial, regional, and cultural histories.

For both of us, the family farm was a shared point of orientation. During our boyhood, there was nothing particularly unusual about that since, although heavily urbanized and industrialized, South Africa retained its links to a dominantly rural and agrarian past. The connection was sustained partly because "the farm" continued to be heavily mythologized and emotionally invested in white South African fiction and culture, perhaps especially that of the Afrikaners, who were, after all, the "boere." In fiction and ideology, the farm could figure as the ground of being for whites: ventriloquizing his youthful self, Coetzee writes in *Boyhood:* "That is what sets him apart: the two farms behind him, his mother's farm and his father's farm. Through the farms he is rooted in the past; through the farms he has substance" (22).

Under the economic conditions of the twentieth century, probably most farms were in fact debt-burdened, marginal operations, yet if anything that only intensified nostalgia for the family farm as the lost paradise. [14] Coetzee's parents were never farmers or landowners—rather, they were impecunious urban residents of the Western Cape with farms only "behind" them—but they had access to family farms (notably Vöelfontein in the Karroo) that left an extraordinarily deep imprint on Coetzee's life and fiction, up to and including *Summertime*. Indeed, in *White Writing* (63–81) Coetzee identified the *plaasroman* (farm novel) as a crucial genre of South African writing in English and Afrikaans, starting in English with Olive Schreiner's *The Story of an African Farm* (1883), another product of Cape bilingualism and biculturalism.

Coetzee distinguishes between the South African farm novel in English, his principal examples being the works of Olive Schreiner and Pauline Smith, and the Afrikaans *plaasroman*, written mainly through the 1920s and 30s, by writers including C.M. van den Heever, Mikro, Abraham Jonker, D.F. Malherbe, Jochem van Bruggen, and Johannes van Melle. In the English farm novel, according to Coetzee, Schreiner and Smith produce, respectively, anti-idyllic and idyllic farm narratives, the one of cultural destitution, suffocation, and attempted flight, and the other of edenic nostalgia in the face encroaching, capitalist modernity. In Afrikaner literary culture, the *plaasroman* occupied more space that did the English farm novel in English literary culture. The antecedents of the English farm novel lie within the country-writing tradition in England, whereas the *plaasroman*'s main affinities are with the German *Bauerroman* of the 1930s, a genre heavily invested in organic rootedness and belonging, and therefore in tune with Nazi ideology. The character Ettinger in *Disgrace*, described as *eingewurzelt* (rooted in), is the last representative, on the verge of extinction, of the European peasant-farmer type in Coetzee's post-apartheid South Africa. The South African *plaasroman* responds primarily to the "crisis" occasioned by the conflict between emergent agrarian capitalism and supposedly immemorial peasant life; in boer South Africa, this crisis entails the mortgaging and loss of family farms, rural depopulation, and the flow of both whites and blacks to the cities.

Coetzee's distinctions—between farm novel and *plaasroman*—are important, but I have invoked the term *plaasroman* more broadly in this book to encompass English farm writing. "The story of the African farm" goes through many permutations in both English and Afrikaans throughout South African literary history right down to the present: "*plaasroman*" supplies a conceptually powerful cover-term. In the *plaasroman*, as Coetzee notes, the ancestral, feudal, white family farm figures as the microcosm of communal order and well being, generally threatened by modernity, urbanization, migration, and the advent of capitalism.

Coetzee places Nadine Gordimer's *The Conservationst* in this *plaasroman* lineage, citing Tony Voss's observation that the typically silent, occluded, black presence in the *plaasroman* returns with a vengeance when an unidentified black corpse is found on the modern "conservationist's" farm [74–81] (readers are set up for a conventional mystery plot that never materializes). The permutations—or progressive unraveling—of the farm novel in South African writing are extensive: in addition to *The Conservationist*, they include Gordimer's *July's People* and Coetzee's *In the Heart of the Country*, *Life & Times of Michael K* [15] and *Disgrace*. The Margot episode in *Summertime* provides another instance. Often ignorant of the farm novel or inclined to dismiss it as only a boer aberration, Coetzee put English readers on notice of the farm novel's significance and revisionary potential; these South African "versions of pastoral" constitute one of the richest veins in South African writing.

Insofar as life began on the farm for both of us—literally so in my case—our lives have been ones of continuing psychic, cultural and geographical displacement. It is practically a cliché that children growing up in rural and provincial isolation not infrequently become avid, precocious readers, gaining imaginative access to richer and more exotic worlds compensating for the limitations of their own. In due course, early literacy may be converted into a material way out through education. Such was the case for both of us. As so often recorded in Anglophone postcolonial memoirs and works of fiction, both literacy and education meant English literacy and education, with England as the distant object of identification and aspiration. In fact, that formation tended to make England the real, while the colonies were its shadow. (The Antiguan Jamaica Kincaid's *A Small Place* vividly attests to that state of affairs.) Yet part of the story here is that of a massive geopolitical reorientation that made America rather than Britain the new imaginative and material destination. For that to happen, a great deal had to change in Britain and America as well as on the periphery, some of which the following pages document. No doubt ours are personal stories, Coetzee's being the important public one, but they also possess a certain typicality for their provincial times and places.

The book comprises five chapters. The first three, "Arrival," "Settling In," and "Flashbacks," depend more on personal recollection than on textual interpretation, but I have found that those two things cannot be separated in my discussion of Coetzee. Kannemeyer's well-chosen phrase, "A Life in Writing," captures the interpenetration of "life" and "literature" in Coetzee's work; *mutatis mutandis*, a similar interpenetration characterizes my own attempt. The next two chapters, "Boyhood" and "*Disgrace*" are memory-infused commentaries on the books named. Selecting only these two books to represent Coetzee's fiction in the middle of nowhere may seem arbitrary or insufficient, although I have referred to other Coetzee works throughout the book. South Africa is present at least by allusion in all Coetzee's books written up to 1999, and *Age of Iron* deals overtly with the township uprising of 1976 and after.[16]

My final chapter comprises a postscript on W*hite Writing* (1988). I have included it for several reasons. First, to reappraise the book as it appeared in the time and context of its publication and also from the vantage point of the present. Second, to convey as well as I can how the book reoriented critical discussion of writing in South Africa in a new international context, and how radically it altered my own sense what "white writing" in South Africa entailed. Third, to read the book as one that criss-crosses repeatedly with Coetzee's fictional production. It illuminates not only the authors Coetzee discusses but also self-reflexively engages with his own undertakings as a writer. In other words, Coetzee as critic does not merely discuss the work of other writers but inhabits their writing positions provisionally, allowing "sympathetic" exegesis of their challenges and accomplishments as writers. *White Writing* surveys some of the roads taken and not taken by Coetzee and his white-writing predecessors. Fourth, despite the book's studious impersonality, I have tried to attend to its personal subtexts; these make it something more than a work of impersonal, academic criticism. In short, it is a complex book , readable alongside as well as apart from Coetzee's autobiographical writings.

I should emphasize here that I do not feel bound to attempt either critical or biographical coverage of Coetzee. That coverage has been supplied by Kannemeyer's biography and by a large body of criticism, notably Derek Attridge's *J.M. Coetzee and the Ethics of Reading*, David Attwell's *J.M. Coetzee: South Africa and the Politics of Writing*, and Laura Wright, Jayne Poyner, and Elleke Boehme ed., *Approaches to Teaching Coetzee's "Disgrace" and Other Works*.[17] Attwell has also written a critical biography, forthcoming from Penguin. My aim is to provide what information and insight I personally can, in the hope that that will make its own small contribution to the Coetzee archive. *Boyhood, Disgrace,* and *Summertime* are the books in which my own recollections and forms of interest are most strongly engaged. I have not included a chapter on *Youth*, since that book covers the period of Coetzee's move to England after graduating from the University of Cape Town. I had not yet met him, and although I am not unfamiliar with the condition of young South African exiles living on the margins in Britain during that time, I have nothing personal to contribute to the narrative of *Youth*. Where I have touched on that book, it I have confined myself to a few pertinent details of Coetzee's authorial self-fashioning at that time, in a somewhat dispiriting literary milieu. In none of this do I purport to offer a definitive South African perspective on Coetzee, if for no other reason than that I left the country in 1974, and am now a US citizen who has lived and worked in America, despite periodic returns to South Africa, ever since. Nor can I speak now, if I ever could, for how Coetzee is read in South Africa as distinct from being read abroad. It is true that Coetzee's work may never have aroused the degree of interest and admiration in South Africa that it has outside the country, despite its early inclusion in some South African university syllabi and despite the very impressive efforts of some critics (cited elsewhere) of South African origin. Certainly, the most negative views of which I am aware, some noted in my final chapter, have come from within the country. What mattered for many South Africans up to the termination of apartheid in 1994 was the relation of fiction being produced in the country to the anti-apartheid struggle. Writers were called upon to engage overtly and make their allegiances clear. Among leading white writers, Nadine Gordimer, South Africa's other Nobel Prizewinner, was not infrequently held up during the 1970s and 80s as the exemplary anti-apartheid novelist in contrast to the "unpolitical" (self-indulgently literary, formalist, allegorical) Coetzee.

Just when one might have thought that topic was exhausted, Imraan Coovadia revived it in his "The Novel in Transition" (2013): [18]

> The fact that there are so few points of contact between Coetzee and Gordimer defined the literary scene in South Africa for three decades . . . Gordimer was close to the ever-new cadres of left wing black and white writers, playwrights, and artists of Johannesburg . . . . In recent years, as Coetzee has eclipsed his older rival as a global figure, it is good to remember that Gordimer's contributions to writing don't necessarily turn up on the page (6).

Generally speaking, pitting Gordimer and Coetzee against each other as rivals served neither, and it set Gordimer up to be ultimately the loser. Having been proclaimed "relevant" under apartheid, she was proclaimed by some to have become "irrelevant" under post-apartheid.

Political allegiance aside, however, there was something palpably "alien" about Coetzee as a writer that initially denied him easy reception in his own country. To this day, there remains something guarded about his South

African welcome. In a letter to me written in 2007, Coetzee mentions that in 2005 then-president Thabo Mbeki awarded him a state prize for achievement "with a tight little smile." Even an admiring, gifted South African critic like Tony Morphet, who has written memorably about Coetzee, could at one time acknowledge Coetzee's singular achievement while confessing his inability to say precisely what was so profound about it: "To all readers, perhaps especially to South Africans, the work was challenging, strange, and difficult when it appeared, and it remains so after nearly thirty years of extended commentary and discussion. Even now, I share the magistrate's baffled realization in *Waiting for the Barbarians*: 'I think: "there has been something staring me in the face, and I still do not see it."'[19] Coovadia might suggest that there is no "it" to be seen, Coetzee's work being, in effect, an artifact of critical theory only, without novelistic substance. Even if that were the case, however, the imaginative realization of critical theory in and as fiction would be no small accomplishment.

Following this brief retrospect, my first chapter will shift to the present tense in which this book had its inception, and which is also the "tense" of many of my recollections of Coetzee. The weave of past and present will, however, continue throughout the book.

NOTES

1. J.M. Coetzee, *In the Heart of the Country* (Johannesburg: Ravan Press, 1978), 50; New York: Penguin, 1982).

2. Teresa Dovey, *The Novels of J.M. Coetzee: Lacanian Allegories* (Cape Town: Donker, 1988), first suggested that *In the Heart of the Country* is Coetzee's rewriting of Olive Schreiner's *The Story of an African Farm* (1883) the Ur-novel of South African Literature in English.

3. Here, I stick to my characterization of the novel as aggressively postmodern, although debate has transpired about whether Coetzee's oeuvre as a whole should be classified as modernist, late modernist, or post-modernist. Some have perceived a turn to realism from at least *Age of Iron* through *Disgrace*. See Jane Poyner, "Contexts and Criticism," ed. Laura Wright, Jane Poyner and Elleke Boehmer, *Approaches to teaching Coetzee's "Disgrace" and Other Works* (New York: Modern Language Association, 2014), 9.

4. *Boyhood* (New York: Viking, 1998); *Youth: Scenes from Provincial Life* (London: Secker & Warburg, 2002); *Summertime: Fiction* (New York: Viking, 2009); *Scenes from Provincial Life: Boyhood, Youth, Summertime* (New York: Penguin, 2012).

5. Jane Tompkins's "Me and My Shadow," *New Literary History*, 19, 1, (1987), 169–78, is generally credited as the founding document of personal criticism; other feminists who followed her lead included Nancy Miller, Mariana Torgovnik, Cathy Davidson, and Alice Kaplan. See Aram Veeser, ed., *Confessions of the Critics* (London: Routledge, 1996).

6. J.M Coetzee, *Dusklands* (Johannesburg: Ravan Press, 1974).

7. J.M. Coetzee, *White Writing: On the Culture of Letters in South Africa* (New Haven: Yale University Press, 1990).

8. J.C. Kannemeyer, *J.M. Coetzee: A Life in Writing* (Cape Town: Jonathan Ball, 2012).

9. See David Attwell, *J. M. Coetzee and the Life of Writing: Face to Face with Time*, forthcoming from Viking, September 2015.

10. Hedley Twidle, *Getting Past Coetzee* (Vintage Digital, 2013).

11. See, for example, the special issue of PMLA, 124, 2 (2009), 361–69, in which Marianne DeKoven among others, citing Coetzee, poses the question "Why Animals Now?"

12. Ingrid Winterbach revisits the scene of the Boer War and the legacy of the camps in the novel *Niggie,* translated into English as *To Hell with Cronjé*, trans. Elsa Silke (Open Letter: University of Rochester, 2010). Set in the last months of the Boer War, the novel is deeply infused with the conventions and experiences of war memoir and fiction in the twentieth century, including post-Vietnam, and it evokes the continuing trauma and loss of the Boer defeat by the British.

13. In a sense, Coetzee solves this problem in *Foe*, where the black character Friday has had his tongue cut out. That atrocity literalizes the "silencing" of black speakers in white representation and, more broadly, in the imperial domain of white writing. (It is, however, a silencing that reignites the master's desire to put words into Friday's mouth or wring speech from his silence.)

14. For whites, the dark underside of the South African farm was perpetual indebtedness to the government Land Bank. For blacks, farm employment often meant virtual slavery and physical assault.

15. J.M. Coetzee, *Life & Times of Michael K* (New York: Penguin, 1985).

16. J.M. Coetzee, *Age of Iron* (New York: Penguin, 1998).

17. Derek Attridge, *J.M. Coetzee and the Ethics of Reading* (Chicago: University of Chicago Press, 2005); David Attwell, *J.M. Coetzee: South Africa and the Politics of Writing* (Berkeley and Los Angeles: University of California Press, 1993); Laura Wright, et al., ed. *Approaches to Teaching Coetzee's "Disgrace."*

18. Imraan Coovadia, "Forum Kritika: The South African Novel in Transition: 1990–2010: Coetzee in and out of Cape Town," *Kritika Kultura,* 18 (2012), 103–15.

19. Tony Morphet, "Reading Coetzee in South Africa," *World Literature Today,* 78, 1 (2004), 14–16.

Chapter One

Arrival

December 2009: the first American edition of J.M. Coetzee's *Summertime: Fiction* (hereafter *Summertime*) appears. My personal curiosity is piqued. Here, it would seem from the publicity, is a fictionalized autobiography that covers the period in which I had overlapped with Coetzee at the University of Cape Town. I do not expect to feature in this "fiction"—why should I?—but I am curious about ways in which my own recall of those years may or may not coincide with Coetzee's fictionalized ones.

I receive a complimentary copy of the book from Viking, with a signed card from Coetzee. Is it a gift or a message? Both? I want to thank him. His University of Adelaide electronic mailbox is full. I send an actual letter, on paper. He replies in an email, "What a pleasure to receive an old-fashioned letter." I read the book. In it, the author John Coetzee has died in Australia. We are being given some materials of a posthumous biography in preparation by a literary biographer.

These materials include a small number of dated notebook entries and some "undated fragments" written, we must believe, by Coetzee between 1972 and 1975. The full time span covered by the book is not, however, wholly clear. Most of the book consists of contemporary "interviews" conducted by the biographer assembling the book. These are interviews with people, all women with one exception, with whom Coetzee is evidently known to have had relationships. The John Coetzee of *Summertime* will thus be a function of heterogeneous memories dating back as much as thirty years.

In the interviews, John is mostly recalled as a lover. His shortcomings in that and other departments are unsparingly reported, but not reported without vividness and a certain continuing respect on the part of the female interviewees. Nothing close to full disclosure is claimed in these interviews or on their behalf by the biographer. Each of the women sets her own limits to what she will reveal, and the composite biography that emerges is hardly scandalous. A memoir—or "summertime" dream—of serial love affairs the book may be, yet it is hardly a Casanova story of serial conquests.

Nevertheless, Coetzee's decision to "recall" these years through a series of romantic episodes stands out. For me, it points to a feature of Coetzee's writing that has, I believe, been the elephant in the room of Coetzee criticism, namely Coetzee's persistent representation, both autobiographical and fictional, of erotic relations and encounters between men and women. It is understandable that critics have not generally thought of Coetzee as a "romantic" writer since the "romances" in question are typically queasy, disturbing, or painful—even shocking—and they are represented with an analytical or confessional stringency generally sufficient to dispel "romance" as ordinarily understood. Nevertheless, the "romantic" commitment persists at least through *Disgrace*, in which the protagonist, Lurie, is not only a womanizer of sorts, as he puts it, but also an academic romanticist who proclaims himself a servant of Eros and quotes Blake and Byron among others on the prerogatives of (male) desire. In the course of the novel, Romanticism seems to fade out, but romance not necessarily so. Moreover, in *Youth*, the young Coetzee links his poetic aspiration to the pursuit and celebration of love, or, rather, links his sense of poetic incapacity to a deficiency of passion. In relation both to provincial South Africa and to metropolitan poetic culture of the 1960s, this romanticist conception of the poet seems strangely anomalous, out of time and out of place, but it also seems like an *idée fixe* that does not easily submit to chastening even as the protagonist turns his hand to prose fiction.

Fictional romance has obviously had an extensive counterpart as nonfiction in Coetzee's life history. Gossip has not been lacking, some of it having to do with Coetzee's relations with, and treatment of, women. Kannemeyer covers some of that history; I shall touch on it briefly in due course. In the nature of things, however, much cannot be known or told, and I have no particular revelations to make here. Coetzee's putative or actual romances will not be my focus in returning to *Summertime*, and I introduce them here both because they are largely the substance of the book and they provide an occasion for flagging the larger general issue of the "romantic" Coetzee.

Summertime, then, is an exercise in "posthumous" fictional autobiography, covering three years of Coetzee's life after his return to take up a teaching post at the University of Cape Town in 1972. Just how fictional the work is can be seen at a glance. The John Coetzee being recalled is single. The historical John Coetzee of 1972–75 was married to Philippa, née Jubber, with two children, Nicolas and Gisela. In some respects, however, *Summertime* turns out to be intensely realistic, especially as regards Coetzee's father Jack, and as regards John's own pained relationship with him up to the moment of Jack's death from cancer in John's care. *Summertime* appears, then, to be returning to some unfinished business. It is another delayed reckoning with a parent and a relationship Coetzee could evidently process only with difficulty, one previous attempt having been made in *Boyhood*. The book thus seemingly acknowledges an obligation, yet again, to come to terms with this long-disavowed parent, an embarrassing and shaming figure, an attorney always represented as a weak, desperate failure under a legal and financial cloud.

Reverting to *Summertime*, I am surprised to recognize myself in the figure of Martin. I don't suggest that I am represented under the name Martin. That interviewee is surely a compound ghost of Coetzee's Anglo-South African academic near-contemporaries of that time, with some invention thrown in.[1] Although Martin is reported as having left South Africa permanently around 1975, he has immigrated to Britain and settled in Sheffield. I, on the other hand, left South Africa permanently in 1974, initially to enter the Ph.D. program in English at Berkeley. Where I recognize myself unmistakably in "Martin" is as the pipe-smoking interviewee at the University of Cape Town in 1972, applying for the same job as Coetzee.

As someone returning from America (that was all I knew about him) Coetzee was exotic. The pipe-smoking academic, such as Martin is and I was, was a relic of the imagined Oxbridge world. My few, earlier prototypes for the faculty member of American origin were generic: first, a historian at my former institution, the University of Natal, whose avowed reason for settling in South Africa was his admiration of the government's racial policies. An American southerner, he had evidently found the Old South reborn in South Africa. (It was he who also caused some amusement by referring to the black subjects of his Natal historiography as "Zulars.") Other American professors, mostly elderly and mostly Southern or Midwestern, would troop by annually to give Fulbright-supported talks. Typically, there would be the Huck Finn lecture and the Moby-Dick lecture. The efforts of these courtly gentlemen merely served to confirm a deep-seated Anglocentric prejudice against the American academy (a prejudice that did, however, begin to crumble in the late 60s as distant rumors of intellectual revolution in the American academy began to reach southern shores).

So here in the foyer I was meeting a South African who had evidently become a type of the new, avant-garde American. Word had certainly spread to South Africa about the revolutionary goings-on in the United Sates during the 1960s and early seventies. In fact, Cape Town had somewhat belatedly plunged into its own Age of Aquarius. A militant, pre-academic feminism had arrived through publications by Germaine Greer (*The Female Eunuch*, 1970), Shulamith Firestone (*The Dialectic of Sex,* 1970), and Kate Millett (*Sexual Politics*, 1970). Connections were frequently made between the war in Vietnam and forms of South African violence and oppression, and those connections were of course unpacked and elaborated in *Dusklands*. Although still fundamentally liberal, the English-speaking white South African academy had become radicalized to a degree: imported terms like "Pigs" and "Feds" now circulated. The academic liberal conscience had increasingly come under critical pressure—from Marxists among others—and was uneasily trying to negotiate its relations with ascendant Black Power.[2]

Although Coetzee arrived in Cape Town carrying some of this baggage, he still seemed alien to me. Coetzee's shoulder-length black hair, casual dress, and reticent manner made him intriguingly different, vaguely countercultural. The slight pallor disapprovingly noted in *Summertime* by his Afrikaner relatives on the farm spoke of northern winters. His air of subdued intensity made it seem as if there might be more to him than met the eye. The tiny red Fiat, left-hand drive, in which I saw Coetzee leave the campus, was not only foreign but would barely have counted as a car in the South African, middle-class reckoning. Ownership of this Fiat, the predecessor of the famous, barebones Datsun truck in *Summertime,* seemed like a gesture of anti-bourgeois austerity, although affordability on an academic pittance probably explained the choice.

My recall of the interview differs in some respects from Martin's.[3] Martin recalls three candidates, one from Stellenbosch University, while I recall only the two of us. I had been invited to interview by David Gillham, the former chair of the English Department in Pietermaritzburg, and was his favored candidate. Some of the Cape Town faculty members doing the interviewing came from departments of foreign languages and Comparative Literature, however, a fact that did not predispose them to favor me as a product of Leavisite mentors, being brought in to advance Gillham's militantly Leavisite program to make over the Cape Town English Department (the multi-volume Cambridge reprint of *Scrutiny* adorned Gillham's study bookshelves).

Being "Leavisite" meant, of course, continuing to implement the critical and pedagogic program launched in 1932 by F.R. Leavis and his *Scrutiny* associates. Akin to the American New Criticism in its emphasis on close reading and the development of literary-critical judgment—the imperatives classically enunciated in America by John Crowe Ransom in "Criticism, Inc." against the prevailing literary historicism—it shared the New Criticism's dedication to what Leavis, quoting T.S. Eliot, called "the common pursuit of true judgment."[4] Leavisite pedagogy and reading practices constituted Practical Criticism, definitionally opposed to literary theory, and intended to cultivate the reader's ability to make moral rather than aesthetic judgments of literary quality.[5] Close reading practices were pursued both through lectures on English canonical texts, "coverage" being the goal of the undergraduate major, and through seminars in which students would be exposed to unidentified samples of English poetry for comparative evaluation and analysis. Others have written about the anxiety accompanying this exercise, since students were called upon to distinguish between "good" and "bad" poems, and shame attached to the choice of the bad poem. Choosing between unidentified and wholly decontextualized examples made these seminars more like an exercise in divination than in judgment, or in seeking cues from the demeanor of the teacher.

Such was the program that had originated at Cambridge University and had been widely institutionalized in England in the period after World War II. It had then been exported through the still existing or former Commonwealth countries, often by British expatriates (a friend recalls being put through her *Scrutiny* paces as an English student in Malaysia in the 1970s!). Not without justification, Kannemeyer dismisses Cape Town's Leavisite regime as dated and simplistic, yet at best it did possess the virtue of focusing close analytical attention on poetic language and of engaging the skills of native speakers and readers of the language (thereby of course placing non-native speakers at a disadvantage). To some degree, the deficits of Leavisite education could be redressed by the study of foreign literature and criticism, as I did as an undergraduate double major in English and Afrikaans-Nederlands. The latter gave access to a wide range of Afrikaans and Netherlandish literature going back to the middle ages, but the program also included the study of philology and historical linguistics, both utterly foreign to English courses. The downside was that the Afrikaans departments were permeated by Afrikaner nationalist ideology, and study of the Afrikaans language was largely dedicated to asserting its uncontaminated European "purity" (in a country in which whites were legally designated as "Europeans" during my childhood!). I gather that nowadays linguists regard Afrikaans as a creolized form of Dutch, i.e., an "impure" product of colonial interaction with non-European people. In any event, Coetzee participated in the English critical seminars, and, ironically, brought with him a power of poetic analysis far superior to that of most card-carrying Leavisites. I was fortunate enough to observe him in action in a course we team-taught, to which I shall return in a moment.

If it seems puzzling that Leavisite militancy could still have flourished in 1972, forty years after the launching of *Scrutiny*, that fact attests partly to the intensity of Leavisite conviction, but also to the persistence of Leavisite mentorship in the former Commonwealth even after its eclipse in Britain. Before 1972, however, I had already developed misgivings about the continuing Leavisite enterprise, and had begun, in fact, to bite the academic hands that had fed me. It was thus with considerable unease that I found myself at once on display as Gillham's protégé *and* confronting interviewers whose different understanding of academic credentials I divined. Inevitably, as I recognized afterwards, these interviewers must have regarded Coetzee as the superior candidate, which he was. Gillham reported to me later that I would be appointed, but he also conveyed that a very rough meeting had ended in a decision to make offers to both Coetzee and me. We were thus to begin simultaneously in February 1972 as lecturers in the department of English.

In *Summertime*, none of this can form part of Martin's recollection. What he does recall is the aftermath of the interview, in which he both speaks and ventriloquizes Coetzee. Asked how the interview went, Coetzee responds:

"Who knows? he says. "Not well."
"Shall we get a cup of tea?"

We then take a dip into Coetzee's consciousness at the time:

He is taken aback. Are the two of them not supposed to be rivals?
Is it permitted for rivals to fraternize?
It is late afternoon, the campus is deserted. They make for the Student Union in quest of their cup of tea. The Union is closed. MJ—that is what he calls you—takes out his pipe. "Ah, well,' he says, "Do you smoke?"
How surprising: he is beginning to like this MJ, with his easy, straightforward manner! His gloom is fading fast. He likes MJ, and, unless this is all an exercise in self-presentation, MJ seems inclined to like him too. And this mutual liking has grown up in a flash!
Yet should he be surprised? Why have the two of them (or the three of them if the shadowy third is included) been selected to be interviewed for a lectureship in English literature, if not because they are the same kind of person with the same formation behind them (formation: not the customary English word, he must remember that); and because both, finally and most obviously, are white South Africans (208)?

I recognize myself in another moment of Martin's recollections. The biographer in *Summertime* mentions that there is no archival record of courses Coetzee taught at the University of Cape Town, but adds that "among Coetzee's papers I did come across an advertisement for a course that you and he offered jointly in 1976 to extramural students."

Martin responds:

Yes, I do. It was a poetry course. I was working on Hugh MacDiarmid at the time, so I used the occasion to give MacDiarmid a close reading. John had the students read Pablo Neruda in translation. I had never read Neruda, so I sat in on his sessions (212).

If I dwell momentarily on this course, it is because on one hand, it engaged Coetzee's close-reading skills and on the other because those skills were now being applied to poets, and poetic contexts, extremely remote from the standard Leavisite ones (which tended to comprise densely-packed lyrics by Donne, Herbert, Milton, Keats, G.M. Hopkins, and D.H. Lawrence while bypassing more "diffuse" poets like Edmund Spenser and Walt Whitman). Without by any means highlighting the fact, Coetzee was ushering in Comparative Literature in place of the taken-for-granted English Literature: the poets I mainly recall him discussing were Pablo Neruda and Zbigniew Herbert.

In fact, we read MacDiarmid and Neruda only to launch the course. To say that I was "working on MacDiarmid" overstates the case: for me, the Scottish Marxist poet Hugh MacDiarmid represented a poetic activism and explicit political militancy which, in a South African context, I was trying to take on board, very much as a novice (meager clues could be gleaned from books like Jean-Paul Sartre's *What is Literature?* and Georg Lukacs's *The Historical Novel*). Such were the fruits of a renewed interest in Marxism in and out of South Africa. Coetzee's presentation of Neruda was consistent with this renewed interest, Neruda then being an icon of the Left. It was with evident feeling and consciousness of the South African setting that Coetzee read these lines from "The Heights of Macchu Picchu":

> Ancient America, bride in her veil of sea,
> your fingers also,
> from the jungle's edges to the rare height of gods,
> under the nuptial banners of light and reverence,
> blending with thunder from the drums and lances,
> your fingers, your fingers also—
>
> I see the ancient being, the slave, the sleeping one,
> blanket his fields—a body, a thousand bodies, a man, a thousand
> women swept by the sable whirlwind, charred with a rain and night,
> stoned with a leaden weight of statuary
>
> Rising to birth with me, as my own brother."[6]

In reading these lines, Coetzee might have seemed to be wearing his political heart on his sleeve, as one was expected to do. Yet that was not strictly the case. In choosing Neruda and Herbert, Coetzee was certainly conscious of their political resonance, but it was a resonance belonging more to the larger global politics and political philosophy of the twentieth century (of which Leavisite pedagogy seemed almost wholly oblivious) than to the immediate South African situation. If anything was required to underline this fact, it was that he did not seem at this time or later particularly inclined to join in student demonstrations and other forms of campus activism. In this respect, he presented a contrast to David Gillham, for example, who, as newly appointed chair of English, had made the news by being dragged by the police from the steps of Jameson Hall, where students were demonstrating. Coetzee seemed faintly scornful of this episode, although it indicated that there was a price to be paid even for liberal protest. Perhaps Coetzee merely wanted to lower the temperature.

It was only later that Coetzee told me the story of his exit from the United States, a story to which his Afrikaner relatives allude in *Summertime*. Word has spread among them that he may have been criminally convicted in the USA, and has in any case left under a cloud. As Coetzee related these events to me, he had been arrested and charged with criminal trespass with forty-five others (the so-called Faculty 45) while occupying a SUNY Buffalo building during the Vietnam War.[7] The lawyer representing them advised them that they would be convicted in Buffalo given the city's poisonous relations between town and gown as well as citizen hostility to anti-war demonstrators. They would, however, be acquitted on appeal.

So it proved for all but Coetzee. His green card application was still in the pipeline, and required the signature of New York Senator Jacob Javits. From the moment of Coetzee's arrest, the application process stopped in its tracks, and he was obliged, along with his family, to leave the USA, with return to Cape Town the only viable option. He returned in 1971. The person most openly upset by this turn of events was Coetzee's wife Philippa, who seemed, far more than he, like a child of the free-spirited American 1960s, now marooned in Cape Town. Coetzee and I never discussed the psychic impact on him (questions about "feelings" were somehow not encouraged) of his ejection from the United States, although the loss of his position at SUNY Buffalo and the possibility of a return to unemployment in Cape Town can hardly have failed to hurt.

I cannot say whether or not arrest in Buffalo soured Coetzee on public demonstrations. The experience may have suggested to him that there were different and, for him, more constructive ways to channel his politics. Finally, Coetzee's return to UCT was no doubt a welcome contrast in some ways to the nightmarishly oppressive American academic-corporate milieu of "The Vietnam Project" in *Dusklands*, with its New Mandarins devising their technologies of domination.[8] In any event, this return to South Africa proved so enormously enabling for Coetzee as a writer that one had to wonder about the "accident" that had brought him back to Cape Town. It is hard to imagine an outcome of this magnitude eventuating from a mere accident.

The whole question of Coetzee's politics (or lack thereof) in and out of his writing has by now been discussed extensively and sometimes acrimoniously, and I have nothing new to contribute. Suffice to say that Coetzee's sensitivity to political nuance, implication, and subtext was fully on display in his readings of poetry, as was by no means always the case in Leavisite or New Critical practice (which was, in fact, political to the core in ways its practitioners chose not to interrogate). What now strikes me most forcibly about Coetzee's teaching of poetry was its deprovincializing mission, one with both political and cultural dimensions. Coetzee's selection of Neruda represented something of an orthodox choice in a global perspective, but not necessarily so in South Africa, where few had actually read or even heard of

Neruda. South Africa was about as far removed as could be from Spanish or Latin American culture, and was still academically centered on "English" literature. Neruda was not a particularly iconic figure in the local anti-apartheid struggle, if he was one at all. Insofar as he was "relevant," in the idiom of the time, he was so in a significantly distanced and mediated perspective. Neruda's grand invocation of lost brotherhood had no ready translation into the language of contemporary anti-apartheid struggle. For Coetzee to familiarize his work in South Africa was one step in the process of imprinting a new global literary map over the English colonial one. (Coetzee himself was so familiar with Neruda that he had amused himself by producing computer-generated "Neruda" poems even before returning to Cape Town.) Moreover, in discussing "The Heights of Macchu Picchu" as well as other poems by Neruda, Coetzee could trace Neruda's antecedents back to European Surrealism, the movement that had notoriously failed to produce any major impact on English poets. How Surrealism *could* be absorbed and repoliticized within a Latin American poetic idiom and sensibility was another important, deprovincializing lesson of the course. Indeed, the deprovincialization of South African literature in English, and of South African public discourse, became one of Coetzee's major tasks both as a writer and public intellectual. If Coetzee's achievement in this respect can fairly be called remarkable, it has nevertheless not been so without producing significant incomprehension and resistance, as is the way of such efforts.

Coetzee's introduction of Zbigniew Herbert was another deprovincializing initiative. At a time of Marxist academic enthusiasm, it was salutary to encounter an Eastern Bloc writer who was neither a Stalinist nor a freedom-loving poster-boy of the U.S. State Department. Instead, Herbert was clearly the product of a difficult, complex, European-Polish history in which Poland had experienced successive occupations by Nazi Germany and the Soviet Union. That culture had generally been rendered invisible by the Manichean Cold War division between Communism and Democracy. Herbert's metapoetic sophistication, long memory, and tightly controlled intensity evidently appealed to Coetzee, as did Herbert's allusive or allegorical subtext of political violence, cruelty, and totalitarian repression.

Coetzee could additionally connect Herbert to Neruda partly via an anti-idealist poetics of the body, then still largely unrecognized by English academics anywhere. That was no small matter: the failure of recognition with respect to poetry corresponded to a more pervasively idealist framework of cultural understanding and literary interpretation, not without political consequences. Both Neruda and Herbert, Neruda above all, gave extended poetic play to the fact of inhabiting a human body, with the attendant pleasures, pains, and perplexities of that condition. Both poets did so with an acute consciousness of the inhuman violence and cruelty of the ideal operating on the body. Herbert's "Apollo and Marsyas" supplies a graphic example:

> tightly bound to a tree
> meticulously flayed of his skin
> Marsyas
> shouts
> before the shout reaches
> his tall ears
> he rests in the shadow of that shout
>
> shuddering with disgust
> Apollo is cleaning his instrument
>
> only apparently
> is the voice of Marsyas
> monotonous
> and composed of a single vowel
> A
>
> in reality
> Marsyas
> tells
> of the inexhaustible wealth
> of his body
>
> bald mountains of liver
> white ravines of aliment
> rustling forests of lung
> sweet hills of muscle
> joints bile blood and shudders
> the wintry wind of the bone
> over the salt of memory[9]

Another, related, Herbert poem Coetzee presented was the "Elegy of Fortinbras." Inhabiting the subjectivity of Fortinbras, Herbert takes his leave of Hamlet-like stardom and an idealizing yet voracious poetic sensibility:

> Anyhow you had to perish Hamlet you were not for life
> you believed in crystal notions not in human clay
> always twitching as if asleep you hunted chimeras
> wolfishly you crunched the air only to vomit
> you knew no human thing you did not know even how to breathe[10]

Fortinbras is about to take over with a busy new administrative program that will include Danish sewer projects and "a better system of prisons," the poetic alternative of using words apparently being unavailing:

> It is not for us to greet each other or bid farewell we live on archipelagos
> and that water these words what can they do what can they do prince

What complicates Fortinbras's bustling determination to get things done, however, is an oddly persistent wish to connect with Hamlet across a bridge of words, as he contradictorily attempts to do in addressing him in the final couplet. In effect, Fortinbras recognizes that he and Hamlet share the predicament of being immersed in words that fail to deliver what they desire from them. "What can they do," not even formally posed as a question, leaves the function of poetry in suspense, to say the least, but it clearly raises the bar for any vocational commitment as a poet.

If Coetzee did not go on to become formally a poet—or hasn't yet done so— it nevertheless seemed clear that for him "reading" poetry also meant thinking about ways to be a poet, even a political poet. That was no doubt a legacy of his early and occasionally continued poetic vocation, and it implied an intimate bond between reading and writing utterly foreign to "practical criticism," one complaint against which was that it blocked rather than promoted poetic production in its adherents. The lessons of poetry were obviously not lost on Coetzee as a prose writer. Nevertheless, it appears that as a translator as well as a teacher he could satisfyingly channel the poetry of others, notably "Ballade van de Gasfitter" by the great Dutch modernist poet Gerrit Achterberg[11] and the Dutch poems he translated in *Landscape with Rowers*.[12] These translations also make amends for his view of the Dutch expressed in *Youth*, and shared by many of his Anglophone and even Afrikaner contemporaries:

> Dutch poetry has always struck him as rather boring . . . if Vinkenoog [a contemporary Dutch poet] is all that Holland can offer, then his worst suspicion is confirmed: that of all nations the Dutch are the dullest, the most antipoetic. So much for his Netherlandic heritage. He might as well be monolingual (77).

Perhaps Coetzee's interest in Herbert prefigured his subsequent dealings with the 1930s Russian poet Osip Mandelstam and with the broader topic of writing under censorship.

That was the challenge for any South African writer under apartheid, although none of Coetzee's books were ever banned. Indeed, Coetzee once observed that if he had anything to fear from censorship, it was not from the apartheid state but from its hypothetical Marxist alternative. Coetzee's rejection of South African censorship, as summarized by Kannemeyer [260–300] remained steadfast and fully articulated, but it differed to a degree from the default position of South African liberal academics, who tended to oppose all censorship in principle, and for whom any participation in the South African censorship was unthinkable. Coetzee recognized that a choice to participate might be justified, as in nineteenth century Russia, as a way to mitigate the more draconian and unenlightened practices of censorship. In 1974, Connie

Mulder, minister of the interior, invited nominations for qualified people to act on censorship committees; that was supposedly a step towards a more liberal and enlightened censorship. Calling the bluff, Coetzee applied and was turned down. Had he been accepted, it is not clear whether he would have felt his bluff called in turn and felt bound to act. On one occasion in 1982, the then director of publications asked Coetzee to write a report on William Burroughs's *Cities of the Red Night* on the tacit understanding that the book would be released. In the report, Coetzee argued that the book was intentionally obscene but not pornographic—its queer sexual encounters apparently being deemed ipso facto obscene but not erotic—and should be passed; he added that at that stage Burroughs was not an inflammatory writer but one who had merely repeated himself for twenty five years. Typically, then, Coetzee engaged seriously with censorship in both thought and practice, enacting a complex relation to the phenomenon even in South Africa, as liberals like myself would never have conceived of doing.

According to Coetzee, Mandelstam's "Stalin Ode" produced a significant crisis of interpretation.[13] Coetzee took issue with those who, like Anna Akhmatova and Nadzedha Mandelstam, claimed that the poem was written under duress, and could not be taken as authentic, a conclusion endorsed by some of Mandelstam's commentators. Implicitly, it was a poem that would never freely have been written, and therefore did not count. Coetzee observed, however, that the poem *had* been written and could not be discounted since it appeared to lack any signs of irony or "insincerity": the question was rather how Mandelstam *could* have written it.

Clearly, according to Coetzee, in a state of alienation, and equally clearly as an interrogation of *how* to write the poem, but not on that account inauthentic. Stalinism entailed a paternalistic psychic structure rather than just a state apparatus that deeply implicated Mandelstam—perhaps as distinct from Akhmatova and Nadzedha—as the poem attests. The "Stalin Ode" was precisely, therefore, a Mandelstam poem, and a considerable one at that, attesting to the sublime horror of the oedipal Father. In effect, Coetzee took issue with the liberal supposition that authentic writing is writing freely produced, a virtual axiom of anti-censorship polemic in South Africa and the "free world."

The clumsy overkill of South African apartheid-era censorship, albeit highly damaging to many writers, had made it an international laughingstock, but the implicit liberal alternative was clearly too facile. Both the historical complexities and the literary constitutiveness of censorship required the detailed if inconclusive examination Coetzee devoted to them in *Giving Offense: Essays on Censorship*.[14] What really is "other" than liberalism, aside from a self-styled and self-caricaturing conservatism, has remained one of Coetzee's abiding questions, continuing to animate an extended critique of liberalism powerfully launched in *Waiting for the Barbarians* (1982). Needless to say, this critique is of a wholly different order from the scornful, wholesale dismissal of "liberalism" by Marxist academics of the time.[15]

NOTES

1. Kannemeyer writes that Martin "is broadly recognizable as Crewe" (226) thereby pinning down the identification more tightly than I felt warranted in doing.

2. Reluctance to negotiate proved to be the political undoing of the aging, authoritarian Alan Paton, South Africa's longstanding white liberal icon. Both the leader of the non-racial Liberal Party, and the world-renowned author of *Cry, the Beloved Country*, he became a figure of reaction, about whose pseudo-archaic fictional representations of Zulu speech Coetzee later wrote in *White Writing*.

3. See also Kannemeyer's account, 225–27.

4. F.R. Leavis, *The Common Pursuit* (London: Chatto and Windus, 1952); John Crowe Ransom, "Criticism, Inc.", Vincent. B. Leitch, et al., ed, *The Norton Anthology of Theory and Criticism*, 2nd. ed. (New York: Norton, 2010), 971–81.

5. Hostility to theory was not necessarily entailed in Practical Criticism, which included I.A. Richards and William Empson among its forebears, but it became increasingly hostile in its pedagogic incarnation.

6. Coetzee must have been using the Nathaniel Tarn translation mentioned in *Youth*. Pablo Neruda, *The Heights of Macchu Picchu*, trans. Nathaniel Tarn (New York: Farrar, Straus & Giroux, 1966), 59, 63.

7. Information supplied by William Offhaus, Special Collections Assistant, SUNY Buffalo: "Coetzee was a member of what is known as the Faculty 45. They were 45 professors who staged a sit-in of the main administration building, Hayes Hall, on March 15, 1970. Though the demonstrations that led up to their sit-in had roots in the anti-war movement, the Faculty 45 were not protesting the Vietnam War. Their goal was to get the Buffalo Police removed from campus, and convince the administration to convene a town-hall type meeting so that both the administration and the students could air their views in a non-violent manner. Since the sit in violated a judge's restraining order on such demonstrations, the faculty members were arrested." See also: http://www.buffalo.edu/UBT/UBT-archives/28_ubtw05/features. Kannemeyer, 198–204, supplies further details.

8. See Noam Chomsky, *American Power and the New Mandarins* (New York: Pantheon, 1969).

9. Zbigniew Herbert, "Apollo and Marsyas," *Selected Poems*, tr. Czeslaw Milosz and Peter Dale Scott (Harmondsworth: Penguin Books, 1968), 82-83.

10. "Elegy of Fortinbras," *Selected Poems*, 98-99.

11. J.M Coetzee, "Gerrit Achterberg's 'Ballade van de gasfitter': The Mystery of I and You," *PMLA*, 92, 2 (March 1977), 285–96.

12. J.M. Coetzee, *Landscape with Rowers: Poetry from the Netherlands* (Princeton: Princeton University Press, 2003).

13. J.M. Coetzee, "Osip Mandelstam and the Stalin Ode," *Representations*, 35 (1991), 72–83.

14. J.M. Coetzee, *Giving Offense: Essays on Censorship* (Chicago: University of Chicago Press, 1997). See also Hermann Wittenberg, "The Taint of the Censor: J. M. Coetzee and the Making of *In the Heart of the Country*," *English in Africa*, 35, 2 (2008), 133–150, on the censorship situation at the time *In the Heart of the Country* was due to be published. Both Coetzee and the local and British publishers expected the book to be banned. This essay also relates how the international publishers Secker and Warburg bumped the local Ravan Press as Coetzee's publishers.

15. Unflatteringly recalled in one guise in *Youth*. Referring to those who write for *The African Communist*, a journal banned in South Africa, Coetzee writes: "Of the contributors, some, to his surprise turn out to be contemporaries of his from Cape Town—fellow students of the kind who slept all day and went to parties in the evening, got drunk, sponged on their

parents, failed their examinations, took five years over their three-year degrees. Yet here they are writing authoritative sounding articles about the economics of migratory labor or uprisings in rural Transkei. Where . . . did they find the time to learn about such things?" (57) For the record, Coetzee was well versed in the writings of Marx and the principal Marxist critics.

Chapter Two

Settling In

The Neruda-MacDiarmid seminar produced one "showdown" between the old order and the new. An academic visitor to the evening class, accompanied by David Gillham, was L.C. Knights, retired King Edward VII Professor of English at Cambridge and Gillham's former Ph.D. mentor at Bristol. Knights was visiting the department for a term both as a friend of Gillham and as one of *Scrutiny*'s founding figures, best known for "How Many Children Had Lady Macbeth,"[1] but whose classic *Drama and Society in the Age of Jonson* (1962) remains in print to this day.[2] Whether Knights knew it or not, his mission in Cape Town was to advance the Leavisite cause. That fact made him an unwelcome visitor in many quarters irrespective of his merits as a gifted and engaging reader.

In fact, the temperamentally gentle, generous, conciliating Knights had inevitably come to a parting of the ways with the *Scrutiny* militants, F.R. and Q.D. Leavis, and was hardly fitted for the militant role.[3] As an academic visitor, Knights was accommodating to a fault, going out of his way to entertain every critical proposition offered in his seminars. In Cape Town, however, the militancy was coming from another quarter. Knights still represented *Scrutiny*. My championship of MacDiarmid on this occasion was a pointed challenge, not, I must admit, generous or in the best of faith, to both Knights and Gillham. Acting out a separation from Leavisite mentors had become an overriding imperative, to which the decencies gave way. Coetzee had no such particular motivation. The Cape Town English Department in which he had studied as an undergraduate was never Leavisite, and by the time he returned to Cape Town from SUNY Buffalo, a Leavisite agenda must have seemed like a quaint anachronism. Wittenberg observes that:

> Coetzee would have found it attractive to work with Ravan [Press's] formidable new editor Mike Kirkwood, an English lecturer like himself and a major revisionist force in South African literary studies. Kirkwood and Coetzee's ideas about literature coincided in many respects, particularly their rejection of Leavisite criticism, the dominant paradigm in the South African academy at the time. Both shared a commitment to new, theoretically inflected modes of reading, and a revitalization of local literature (146).

Coetzee's arrival thus marked and contributed to a fundamental shift in South African English Studies. The Buffalo luminaries of Coetzee's time included Leslie Fiedler, C.L. Barber, Lionel Abel, Eugenio Donato, and Al Cook, while visitors included Dwight MacDonald, Donald Barthelme, Angus Fletcher, Jerome Mazzarro, Irving Feldman, William Sylvester, Robert Hass, René Girard (a significant presence in some of Coetzee's early criticism)[4] Michel Foucault, Olga Bernal, Lucas Foss, and Hélène Cixous.[5] Knights thus represented something to which Coetzee had little connection and in which he had no live interest; he evinced little more than cool disdain for Knight's intellectual overtures.

In fact, Coetzee's professional experience made it possible for him to recognize and "place" academic visitors far more effectively than I could. On one occasion, for example, the speaker was a leading Dutch Marxist by the name of Kwant, whose mere billing as a Marxist was enough to confer on him a radical celebrity in a country in which real or imaginary Marxists had for so long been silenced and hunted down. The talk that followed presented Marx mainly as an avid, comprehensive reader, somewhat at variance with the expected representation of the revolutionary Marx. If this talk came as a revelation to some, it did not to Coetzee, who considered it run of the mill academic. On another occasion, a visitor to the English Department was a highly touted English medievalist. Either being or posing as *louche* English gentry, he gave a narcissistic, off the cuff performance of the kind no longer really tolerated in the American academy, as Coetzee tersely conveyed. In a word, Coetzee served by both precept and example as a professional mentor in the English Department, in which norms of professional competence and decorum were far from being well established. This was not simply a fault of the Cape Town English Department. At the time, professionalization was still very much a work in progress in South Africa and even in Britain; becoming more fully professionalized inevitably meant assimilating American professional norms and protocols. Coetzee was the herald of this development.

How, then, was Coetzee placed in the divided Cape Town English Department? Punctilious to a fault, he not only did the job but also worked to align the Cape Town English Department with some of the enlightened norms of undergraduate education in America and elsewhere. That included syllabus reform, one manifestation of which was the introduction of the professionalized *Norton Anthology of Poetry*, thereby ending the era of the

Golden Treasuries of "English" verse. It was not Coetzee's style to be confrontational or uncooperative, but for much of the time he remained frostily distant and withdrawn, absent, so to speak, in the department as well as socially. This distance generated anxiety: people felt judged by him and found wanting, whether he was judging or not. Without seeking the role, Coetzee became a focus of disaffection in the department.

Although he practically never discussed his own undergraduate experiences as a Cape Town English student, he had studied in a department divided between Literature and Language. The Arderne literature professor was R.G. Howarth, not without distinction on the Australian literary scene and a competent scholar.[6] In South African Leavisite legend, however, Howarth presented the sorry spectacle of a benighted and deadening scholarly mediocrity. He enjoyed no repute as a spellbinding, charismatic lecturer, such lecturing then representing the gold standard in South African humanities departments. Coetzee, however, became Howarth's protégé and M.A. student, retaining his respect for him; he once expressed admiration for Howarth's ability to extract from his files a professionally competent lecture on practically any topic in English literature. In his memoir *Youth*, Coetzee comments apropos Howarth that "he has nothing against pedants. He prefers them to showmen" (27). Coetzee's own "dry" lecturing, of which undergraduates were generally not enamored, manifested this preference. This was not necessarily a temperamental preference alone. Charismatic, authoritarian lecturing had become—all too briefly, some would say—a casualty of the academic revolution. More than almost any other contemporary writer, however, Coetzee recognized the fictional pleasures and potentialities of "pedantry." An ironized pedantic prissiness of expression and intellectual disposition became a constant resource of his fiction, with obvious appeal to a literate readership.

As a passive focus of disaffection, Coetzee resisted the Leavisite makeover of the Cape Town English Department. In 1973, Gillham engineered the hiring of Trevor Whittock, author of *A Reading of "The Canterbury Tales,"* to the chair of English Language.[7] Whittock had been seared by his experiences at Makerere University, Uganda, under the grisly regime of Idi Amin (rumor had it that the university president had been decapitated, and his head sent back to his family). Whittock was both a political conservative and a militant Leavisite, intellectually descended from the medievalist John Spiers at Essex (reputed to have said that no Arab student would ever be admitted to his dormitory). Whittock's credentials as a professor of language carried weight only with Leavisites, for whom it was enough to have written a book on a Middle English poet to count as a specialist in language. His appointment was contentious. Whittock was, in any event, out of his depth in the academic waters in which he found himself, and his aggressive conservatism placed him at odds with many department members including Coetzee. On one occasion he proposed in a department meeting that students should read Winston Churchill's *My Early Life* as a literary masterpiece. Coetzee intervened deadpan to say that if students were to read books of that type, they would be better off reading the real thing, namely *Mein Kampf*. Coetzee was equally cutting towards another colleague who plaintively interjected the question, "Yes, but what about Beauty?" into every discussion of departmental pedagogy. The discourse of Beauty had, of course, by then succumbed to the militant advance of Theory even if it has made something of a comeback now. Yet Coetzee was not so much an enemy of the aesthetic as of the preciousness of institutionalized poetic "appreciation."

Coetzee never made his peace with the English Department in which he had been hired, but he did express satisfaction at the prospect of Gillham's successor in the Arderne chair. In a letter to me, dated 12/8/1986, he wrote:

> I understand that a black man named Njabulo Ndebele has been offered Gillham's chair. I have a review of N's book in a December issue of *New Republic*. I think the appointment is a thoroughly good idea, but am dubious that N will take up (or be allowed by the comrades to take up) the appointment. I will write from S.A. and tell you how the story develops.

At this point, I do not particularly recall what Coetzee taught in Cape Town. In the interview recorded in *Summertime*, he is asked "what authors would he like to teach? "I can teach pretty much across the board," he replies, "I am not a specialist. I think of myself as a generalist" (206). Later: "Would he feel competent to offer tutorials in Middle English?. . . The truth is, he does not really want this job. He does not want it because in his heart he is not cut out to be a teacher. Lacks the temperament. Lacks zeal." (207). Coetzee could, in fact, teach "pretty much across the board," as faculty were normally expected to do. The reported lack of enthusiasm for teaching somewhat belies the reality but it is not wholly fictional. A flat classroom affect was the apparent result. That had little practical consequence at a time when Cape Town students had just begun to agitate for student course evaluations. In a letter dated 2/12/1983, he wrote:

> I'm on sabbatical leave till June, and having a good time. I have really had my fill of the English Department, and every day I am not there is a day I feel to be rescued from time. There are tentative moves afoot to establish a Comp. Lit. department [in Cape Town], but if that ever comes about it will take years. I'd be happy to make the move. The idea would be that it would teach bread and butter African Literature courses at an undergraduate level, and proper comparative literature only at fourth-year level and beyond.

These plans partly materialized, with what benefit to Coetzee I do not know. In *Summertime,* at all events, Martin reports that Coetzee has said he should have been a librarian, a more congenial choice. Coetzee could be even more antinomian than that; on one occasion he mentioned running an automotive junkyard as his dream job. He even entertained the fantasy of succumbing to a prolonged, "interesting," illness. What *Summertime* leaves out of the picture, however, is that for certain students, usually ones destined for graduate school, Coetzee was the all-important mentor, not just uniquely qualified to prepare them for graduate study but radiating a negative charisma that made him an object of continuing fascination. As time went on and Coetzee's fame expanded, so did the circle of fascination. It became a game for me to see how many minutes it would take in any conversation among writers and literary academics in South Africa before Coetzee's name came up, after which he would remain the topic.

In the classroom, I remember only one lecture, on Henry James's *Washington Square*, in which Coetzee not uncharacteristically emphasized the distinction of the writing. He did teach other American texts in one context or another, Faulkner's among them, the influence of Leslie Fiedler being in evidence, as was that of contemporary psychoanalysis. All this was still relatively novel in South African English Departments. In those departments, *English* had been very much the operative word, and coverage of American texts remained thin and sporadic, largely confined to the few texts regarded as having made it into the great English tradition. In fact, American literature was still treated practically as an English colonial literature.

I team-taught an M.A. seminar with Coetzee on poetry and theory. It was in this course that Coetzee laid out the principles of Saussurean linguistics, hitherto unknown to me and everyone else in the room. This was the time in which a terrifying maxim had begun to gain currency: "Your criticism can be no better than your linguistics." We were now to learn what it meant: The Structure of the Sign; Signifier/Signified; Arbitrariness; A System of Differences without Positive Terms; Linguistic Value as exchange value; Syntagmatic vs. Associative Relations; The coming Science of Semiology; etc. Such was the advent of Theory in the Cape Town curriculum. I believe Roland Barthes' *Mythologies* and Roman Jakobson's analysis of Metonymy and Metaphor supplied the demonstrations in practice. All this notwithstanding, and *pace* Jonathan Culler, "structuralist poetics" remained a virtual oxymoron to me. That changed with the arrival of Jacques Derrida's *Of Grammatology* in English translation in 1976. "Poststructuralist poetics" was a different story, but not, I believe, one Coetzee ever found particularly congenial. In a letter dated 2/12/83, he wrote:

> I've been working on a longish essay on confessions, which I thought would be finished last year, but has only just emerged in a draft that bears reading. It turns out to be an essay on the deferral of truth, but I feel so little qualified to manage the whole of Derrida on one hand, and so reluctant to take on the

hermeneutics of psychoanalysis on the other, that the entire critical strategy inevitably looks naïve . . . it deals with Tolstoy (*The Kreutzer Sonata*), Rousseau (the *Confessions*), and Dostoevsky (*Notes from the Underground, The Idiot, The Possessed*). I did an enormous amount of reading for it, or at least as much as the local library sources allow, though I probably missed major things for lack of anyone to talk to who knows the field.

This reading represented at least the beginnings of Coetzee's profound interest in confessional writing. When Coetzee delivered this paper at Johns Hopkins, ca. 1984, his interest appeared focused on the Russian writers, somewhat at Rousseau's expense, partly because those writers were not, as Rousseau was, incarnations of the European secular Enlightenment. Indeed, Coetzee regarded them as having run the gauntlet of European radical skepticism and come out somewhere on the other side. That fact appears to have made the great Russians exemplary for Coetzee. For him, that fact about them had formal, fiction-writing implications as well as philosophical ones; from his perspective, the Russian writers had more compellingly practiced confessional writing as a theological genre than Rousseau had.

I assume but do not know that Coetzee had initially been drawn to linguistics during the linguistic turn of the 1960s, oversold at the time as another Copernican Revolution. Books on linguistics appeared in quick succession. One of Coetzee's erstwhile Cape Town students, now a prominent American academic, recalled to me that he had encouraged her to study linguistics at Oxford, advice that certainly made sense at the time although it now seems almost quaint. Yet Coetzee's interest in linguistics was fine-grained, both highly technical and professional, not merely a transient investment in the structuralist paradigm, as it was for most academics. His interest in San languages was that of a serious linguist and grammarian. He evidently knew French, German, and Russian, as well as having excellent Dutch and Afrikaans.

Indeed, the deepest cognitive and epistemological issues in Coetzee's writing are seldom far removed from subtleties of grammatical tense, mood and aspect. Attention to such detail, bordering on the fetishistic, is a feature of Coetzee's work that has now been extensively recognized; his work thus solicits particularly attentive, informed close reading. For example Patrick Hayes notes that in *Disgrace*, David Lurie reflects on his professorial role in "explaining to the bored youth of the country the distinction between drink and drink up, burned and burnt. The perfective, signifying an action carried through to its conclusion." [8] These are not merely classroom technicalities but the temporalities through which Lurie's examined life transpires.

For Coetzee, these refinements are of the essence, and they bear strongly on questions of translation, on which topic Coetzee's essays range from Newton's *Principia* in Latin and English respectively to Alan Paton's pseudo-translation from Zulu into English in *Cry, the Beloved Country*.[9] On one occasion Coetzee expounded to me the different and, at one level, untranslatable tense-structures of English and Afrikaans. Strict untranslatability did not, however, deter Coetzee from translating Dutch poetry or Wilma Stockenström's Afrikaans fictional tour de force, *Die kremetartekspedisie* (*The Expedition to the Baobab Tree*).[10] Insofar as Coetzee might have aspired to be a writer in Afrikaans, this book may have stood in for the unwritten Afrikaans novel. The book's attractions for him presumably included the sophisticated first-person narrative of an African slave woman somewhat indefinitely located in historical time and place although the location seems to be east African. She has some of the qualities of a first-person "Coetzee" protagonist. In both its high and colloquial registers, the prose of the novel is taxing, but Coetzee's command of the language is superior, and certainly equal to the challenge of this translation. I do not, however, believe that writing in Afrikaans himself can have been a serious option for Coetzee. He is thus misleadingly called an "Afrikaans writer" in some works of reference.[11]

In *Summertime*, cousin Margot reflects:

> His Afrikaans is halting; she suspects her English is better than his Afrikaans... She blames the deterioration in his Afrikaans on the move to Cape Town, to an 'English' school and an 'English' university, and then to the world abroad, where not a word of Afrikaans is to be heard. *In 'n minuut*, he says: in a minute. It is the kind of solecism Carol will latch on to at once and parody (93).

The fluent direct speech in Afrikaans attributed to John elsewhere in this chapter makes it improbable that he would perpetrate so glaring a solecism (Anglicism), but a certain lack or loss of effortless fluency tallies with my own recollection. Coetzee admired the un-stuffy colloquial brio of the poetry written in Afrikaans by his contemporary Breyten Breytenbach, who makes an appearance in *Summertime*, but did not try to emulate it.

John and cousin Margot recall Afrikaans as the medium of their preoedipal childhood intimacy on the family farm of Voëlfontein in the Karroo—a cousin-love apparently tinged with incestuousness in the eyes of the Afrikaner elders, and the ideal prototype, according to John, of all subsequent, inevitably disappointing loves—and they continue to speak it to one another. Yet the English acculturation of which Margot complains has been decisive. Such, too, is my conviction. At the time Coetzee began writing in earnest, Afrikaans can no longer really have been an option, even before any considerations could arise about a global readership, as they obliquely do through Margot's observation that "not a word of Afrikaans is to be heard" in the world abroad.[12]

This loss of native Afrikaans, whether primarily real or imagined, sets up some identity questions for Coetzee in *Summertime* and elsewhere. He is not strongly English-identified in any South African sense in fiction, and is not in fact, but in *Summertime* the exchange with Margot poses the question whether he is or is not an Afrikaner. He no longer passes for one in his extended family even though Afrikaans is their medium of exchange. Then again, as Margot notes, the criteria of admission to "real" Afrikanerhood have become increasingly restrictive under apartheid (certainly excluded were the "colored" people who were native speakers of Afrikaans). Not a real Afrikaner, then, but forever a self consciously alien and alienated inhabitant of the English language.

For the Afrikaner family members on the farm, John's single condition and failure to "read" as a real (Afrikaner) man immediately and predictably raise the question whether he is a *moffie* (Afrikaans slang for a gay man). In the world of the Karroo family, you are or you aren't, and that becomes the point in debate about John between the sisters Margot and Carol. While Carol, a wealthy middle class resident of Sandton near Johannesburg, alludes mysteriously to certain "advanced" sexual notions governing conduct in her circle, they would seem to govern only heterosexual conduct. In the terms in which Carol and Margot pose the question, which is not simply one of sexual practice but also of social positioning and persona, Margot's denial that John is a *moffie* seems justified, both in the book and in real life.

Linguistic loss and, or as, mortality are registered in another, ostensibly non-personal, way in *Summertime*. John must try to explain to Margot why he has a technical and professional interest in the virtually extinct San and Khoi languages. In South Africa, many of these languages now survive only in the grammars compiled by nineteenth century missionaries. Not without reason, Margot inquires whether John knows isiXhosa, the living language of one of the largest black ethnic communities in South Africa, and the dominant one in the Cape Province. In this respect a typical white South African of his generation, John does not. Yet he denies any need for him to learn isiXhosa, since it is not endangered: the only languages he wishes to acquire are lost ones.[13] Why? "You can speak with the dead . . . who otherwise are cast out into everlasting silence" (104). Before giving this answer he hesitates: "as if the words might be too much for her and even for him." Awesome.

As I became better acquainted with Coetzee and his intellectual repertoire, it was increasingly borne in on me that his having completed an American Ph.D. trumped what could then count as an academic credential in South Africa. Growing acquaintance with Coetzee, although not with him alone, made it increasingly clear to me that I needed to go elsewhere. Support for graduate and research studies in English in South Africa was inadequate. Such studies were not, and could not be, a high priority in a country with far more pressing social needs. Moreover, by 1974 it had become evident that the scene of the real intellectual action in English studies—and possibly in the domain of social change—was the United States. The prospect of relocating to England was not exciting, and it carried the additional risk of permanently accepting—or vainly seeking to overcome—one's status as a "colonial."[14] Here again, Coetzee supplied a model. Unlike practically all his South African academic contemporaries, Coetzee gave little credit to Englishness as such, either in South Africa or abroad. His own Afrikaner affiliations distanced him both from the Anglo provincialism of South Africa and from the entrenched snobbery of Anglo-South Africans with respect to Afrikaners. This un-Englishness came as a liberating surprise to me, the effect of which was reinforced by Coetzee's multilingual literary cosmopolitanism, unequalled in my previous experience. That un-English cosmopolitanism, as well as his immersion in American culture, would contribute to Coetzee's decisive makeover of "South African Literature" in English.

DUSKLANDS

My first inkling of Coetzee's productive intellectual life came from a visit to his study at home. On the wall, a pin-board recorded his works in progress as well as the publications for which they were destined. This systematic approach was novel to me, still largely unacquainted with what academic productivity meant in the United States. In a later letter, dated 2/12/1983, Coetzee had this to say: "It was only after a couple of years at Buffalo that that it dawned on me that people around me were not just writing random critical articles, that there was an overall conception in each case of where an article would fit into a future book. I'm far from that position myself, though I would really like to write a book of criticism" (the book that later emerged as *White Writing*).

The first publication by Coetzee that I read was an article published in *Computers and the Humanities* on Samuel Beckett's *Lessness*.[15] Both the publication venue and the critical approach could hardly have struck me as more outlandish. (Was it a parody?) The article sought to elicit the mathematical rules of a "combinatorial game" (198) that, in Coetzee's view, governed the recursive structure of Beckett's minimalist text. At a later time, Coetzee's *Youth* would supply an account of his undergraduate mathematical training and subsequent employment in the British computer industry; both a professional familiarity with mathematics and access to the "primitive" computer resources of the time provided the basis for Coetzee's analysis of *Lessness*. The mathematics involved were wholly beyond me, and Coetzee loftily made no concessions to humanistic incapacity. Perhaps, at one level, that intransigence was aggressively the point. Some humanists took the bait.

In *Youth*, Coetzee recalls that, when he published computer-generated poems in in a Cape Town literary magazine, they were framed by a derisive editorial commentary. "For a day or two back in Cape Town, he is notorious as the barbarian who wants to replace Shakespeare with a machine" (161). I recall similar collegial reactions to the essay on *Lessness*: was it to this that the humanities had come? Yet for me the lure of the paper outweighed the threat it presented. It had seemingly cracked the code of a text—and to some degree of a major postmodern author—that would either have remained illegible under the regime of "practical criticism" or been mindlessly dismissed as nihilistic. Moreover, while denying that *Lessness* was an expressive text—rather, it was an enclosed set of combinatorial games—Coetzee reflected on the epistemological and existential consequences that ineluctably followed from Beckett's procedure. He thereby paradoxically credited *Lessness* with its own expressive power. No question that important reading lessons were being taught here, although in hindsight it is also possible to infer that *Lessness* must have taught Coetzee an important writing lesson, on writing as "decomposition'—undoing and dismantling—rather than "composition." The spareness of his novels sometimes makes them seem like products of subtraction rather than addition.

Somehow, I gathered that Coetzee had also completed a fictional manuscript. Either he asked me to read it or, more likely, I asked to read it, despite the usual misgivings about possibly not liking a colleague's work and having to find something nice to say. The manuscript I received was that of *Dusklands*, already complete. It was a slender ms. typed in a modern, square font unfamiliar enough in South Africa to look hip. My interest thus piqued, I began to read. Within ten pages, my astonishment could hardly have been greater.

In fact, for me this reading was the once-in-a-lifetime experience of encountering an unpublished work that immediately seemed to me extraordinary, game changing, off-scale. Having expected to feel no more than the tepid or qualified interest to which I, like many of us raised on the English canon, were accustomed in responding to South African fiction in English, on this occasion I found myself deeply excited by the quality of the prose and by the decidedly new sensibility and frame of reference evinced by the book. Without, of course, foreseeing the book's breakout into the world market, let alone the books to follow or the Nobel Prize not yet on the horizon, I formed an absolute conviction of the book's importance. I felt impelled to record this conviction by writing a review of *Dusklands* before it was published, a review that then appeared, after publication of the novel, in the South African literary journal *Contrast*.[16] I believe this was the first review ever published of a work by Coetzee.

The review, which readers may of course consult if they wish, was written according to my lights at the time. It noted Coetzee's affinities with

Beckett, Nabokov, Borges, and other writers who comprised the postmodern canon. If I did not label the book postmodern, it was because the term was not widely circulated by 1972, and was still unknown to me. The review noted the derivation of the title *Dusklands* from Spengler's *Abendländer*. It noted the intersecting forms of violence in nineteenth century South Africa and twentieth century America, both arising from the imperial projection of power, extension of the "frontier," and the self-aggrandizement of the masculine subject of power. It enthusiastically proclaimed the work unprecedented in South African writing. It made a point of Coetzee's exotic range of reading and intellectual reference among South African writers. It drew attention to irreconcilable narrative inconsistencies that I had only just learned to read as the metafictional sign of fictiveness as such. This was the substance of the review.

From the moment of its publication, *Dusklands* was out of my hands, so to speak, and in the public domain. One immediate reaction came from a professor in Philippa's department, who commiserated with her on being married to such a madman. No doubt other "normal" white South Africans shared that reaction. Among more practiced readers, however, *Dusklands* soon began to garner critical attention that increased exponentially as Coetzee continued to publish. The international publisher Secker and Warburg as well as Ravan in South Africa published Coetzee's next novel, *In the Heart of the Country*; Penguin picked up *Dusklands* in 1985. Coetzee had decisively become a global writer.

At this point, there are certainly other things I would emphasize about *Dusklands*, among them its virtual reconstitution of the category of "South African Literature." The projected readership of *Dusklands* was global, cosmopolitan, contemporary, sophisticated. It was not the first South African novel to make an international impact: Olive Schreiner's *The Story of an African Farm* and Alan Paton's *Cry, The Beloved Country* had already done so. Paton established the anti-apartheid narrative as the paradigmatic South African one in English. Yet despite and even because of these successes, South African Literature remained a respectable colonial subset of English literature, supported by the most banal discourse of its history (Olive Schreiner, Pauline Smith, Roy Campbell, Alan Paton, early Nadine Gordimer), aesthetic claims, and local peculiarities. Tellingly, English departments hardly deigned to notice it, even when written by the likes of Schreiner and Paton (to say nothing of writers of color like Alex La Guma and Eski'a Mphahlele). The category began to crumble, but not yet fall, with advent of writers like Athol Fugard and Douglas Livingstone as well as black writers like Mongane Wally Serote. Sol Plaatje's neglected *Mhudi* began to receive overdue attention.

Coetzee's substitution of "writing" for "literature" made a decisive cognitive breakthrough. "Literature" begged the question unproductively, as did

South African identity, and the term "literature" came, in fact, to seem questionable in many fields in the wake of deconstruction. To the picture of "white writing," Coetzee insisted on adding the Afrikaans writers C.M van den Heever and Mikro as well as the now non-canonical Sarah Gertrude Millin. Coetzee also introduced the new categories of the picturesque and the sublime in relation to nineteenth century South African nature poetry, and of the farm novel (*plaasroman*), a major genre of South African white writing in both Afrikaans and English. All this reconstituted *his s*ense of his South African precursors and options, but also suspended "South African Literature" as a provincializing denomination.

Finally, one feature of *Dusklands* of which I failed to appreciate the full significance was its mining of the South African archive rather than South African literature for fictional materials. In *Youth* (137–39) Coetzee records the excitement of discovering William Burchell's *Travels in the Interior of Southern Africa* a two-volume work that appeared in 1822 and 1824.[17] Writing from within its historical horizon immediately appeals to Coetzee, as does the "real" it represents. Other materials were to be found, *inter alia*, among the extensive publications of the Van Riebeeck Society, founded in 1918 and still active. [18] (The publications of this society included narratives in various European languages of travel, exploration, and penetration into the interior; it was through parody and fictionalization of the historical text that Coetzee produced his "Narrative of Jacobus Coetzee" in *Dusklands*.)[19] The protagonist, a fictional ancestor, penetrates into the interior with a vengeance, both geographically and psychically.

In a sense these materials supplied Coetzee with the answer to the question where and how to begin writing in earnest. Merely seeking to imitate dead masters like Henry James or Ford Madox Ford, both of which efforts lead to a dead end in *Youth*, had proven to be no solution to the problem of beginning. Nor had the attempt to find the source of poetry within, in the guise of romantic passion. The archive supplied both an imitable narrative form and a habitable fictional persona, that of the nineteenth century ancestor/explorer/colonizer Jacobus Coetzee. This, as far as I am aware, was a radically new and ambitious use of a somewhat arcane South African archive billed (and used or underused) primarily as a historical source. Looking back, one cannot but wonder whether "The Narrative of Jacobus Coetzee" heralded a broader cultural turn to untapped historical archives, including photographic and media archives, with a corresponding defection from fiction made up out of imaginative whole cloth or even through literary imitation alone. *Dusklands* certainly broke new ground that Coetzee could continue to exploit.

Coetzee's exploitation of the historical archive extended, however, to parodic revision of the literary archive that included innumerable Western and South African fictions of exploration, adventure, hunting, and colonial encounter, often brutal and bloody, with the Other. Coetzee's familiarity with this archive is apparent throughout *Dusklands*, but it is almost a hyperfamiliarity that enables him to boil down the options with ironic mastery in his rendering of the encounter with the "Hottentots" (Khoikoin):

> Tranquilly I traced in my heart the forking paths of the endless inner adventure: the order to follow, the inner debate (resist? submit?), underlings rolling their eyeballs, words of moderation, calm, swift march, the hidden defile, the encampment, the gray-bearded chieftain, the curious throng, words of greeting, firm tones, Peace! Tobacco! demonstration of firearms, murmurs of awe, gifts, the vengeful wizard, the feast, glut, nightfall, murder foiled, dawn, farewell, trundling wheels ... the contest of magic, the celestial almanac, darkness at noon, victory, an amusing but tedious reign as a tribal demigod....[20]

Clearly, knowledge is power as the European celestial almanac allows the whites, as in Rider Haggard's *King Solomon's Mines*, to anticipate the eclipse that creates panic among the natives. Despite the satirical inflection of this passage, however, Coetzee makes the "heroic" narrative of discovery and colonial encounter—like narratives of Vietnam—an almost hallucinatory projection of the "inner adventure" of the Western self. It is an adventure in which the Other will, on one hand, become an elusive figment (as in *Waiting for the Barbarians*), and, on the other, be pursued with genocidal fury for failing to conform to the inordinate demands and contradictory wishes of the Western self.

The Jacobus Coetzee narrative can certainly be read as a devastating critique of colonialism, but the hubris of the protagonist (in fact, of both protagonists in *Dusklands*) is not without tragic potentiality. In discussing Sarah Gertrude Millin in *White Writing* (136–62), Coetzee perceives a tragic dimension in her writing, one generally absent in South African writing. For Millin, what creates the possibility of tragedy in a "post-religious" age, and in South Africa, is the phenomenon of miscegenation, resulting in "mixture" within the pure bloodline. Drawing heavily on the late nineteenth and early twentieth century pseudoscientific discourse of "degeneracy," Millin represents the mingling of blood as always catastrophic, and always fated to betray itself in the line of descent, no matter how "white" the offspring may seem to become. Such is the secular instantiation of the biblical maxim that the sins of the fathers will be visited on the children. No such conception of fatedness is available to Coetzee, but the "megalomania" to which critics have alluded can also be called hubris, and in both "The Narrrative of Jacobus Coetzee" and, later, *Disgrace* the protagonist passes through an extreme process of mortification in which he is humiliated, stripped, denuded, and perhaps, to a limited degree, enlightened. That process might seem gratuitous without the initial condition of hubris. In the "Narrative," what is more, the protagonist performs his own literal catharsis by expelling the pus from a rectal abscess he has developed. In the inverted oedipal scenario of *The Vietnam Project*, a father, to whom the term "insane" might well apply, stabs the son he loves in what seems almost like a somnambular state. All this is consistent with the critique of colonialism, but these quasi-tragic perspectives do not belong to that critique in either its liberal or radical guises. They entail both literary consciousness and a degree of identification with the perpetrators. No wonder the book offended anti-apartheid activists. Although Millin would now generally be dismissed because of her racial ideology and her support during the 1960s for the grand architect of "separate development," H.F. Verwoerd, Coetzee provides a surprisingly sympathetic account of her, arguing that the abhorrent discourse of degeneracy supplied her with a template and materials for writing, always a legitimate and even overriding consideration for Coetzee, as it would seldom be for critics of apartheid or colonialism. Millin found a way of filling the "empty" space of white writing in South Africa.

Obviously, a great deal more can be, and has now been, said about the book, either standing alone or in the broader context of Coetzee's mature oeuvre. It is undoubtedly possible, especially in the retrospect afforded by Coetzee's other books, to be conscious of a certain immaturity and mannered ostentation in *Dusklands* as a feat of style, as well as its palpable indebtedness to fashionable authors of the time. The book-jacket blurb on the most recent Vintage edition of *Dusklands* includes the comment that "His writing gives off whiffs of Conrad, of Nabokov, of Golding, and of the Paul Theroux of *Mosquito Coast.*" This off the cuff observation hardly represents scholarly engagement with *Dusklands*' precursors and intertexts, but it does articulate the experience of readers who find these "whiffs" more intrusive than merely allusive. Part of the overkill can be attributed to Coetzee's desire to make his mark in the field of contemporary writing, but his subsequent fiction generally reveals a formal mastery of his situation still lacking in *Dusklands*. For what it is worth, engaging critically with *Dusklands* at the time of its appearance was a significant exercise for me at a moment when I almost desperately needed to find my place and find my way.

As regards the current reception of *Dusklands*, Vintage's decision to reissue the book in 2014 implies a conviction of its continuing importance and marketability, although no doubt now as a function of Coetzee's general preeminence. Again, the blurb to this edition probably speaks for a rough consensus:

> The unflinching sense of loss, the claustrophobic acknowledgement of the unwilling interdependence of master and slave, and its subtle prose style make it an extraordinary achievement (*Sunday Times*).

> Both the eighteenth century Jacobus Coetzee and the twentieth century Eugene Dawn are in the business of pushing back the frontiers of knowledge and are dealers in death who denounce [renounce?] their own humanity and spurn their feelings of guilt. In these two narratives, Coetzee has crystallized in their absurdity and horror the extremes of scientific evangelism and heroic exploration.

From the moment of its publication, *Dusklands* positively cried out for theoretical approaches, which it had indeed anticipated and incorporated.[21] (The first of these was Teresa Dovey's *The Novels of J.M. Coetzee: Lacanian Allegories*, which established the dialectic of master and slave as a key structuring template for both narratives in *Dusklands*, as it would remain through *In the Heart of the Country*). Yet theoretical (aesthetic, ethical) approaches then and now do not necessarily capture the "horror" to which the book attested in its time. Readers may find this comment puzzling since *Dusklands* might seem to articulate a surplus of "horror," but the "horror" in question entailed forms of shock, disorientation, and trauma that belonged both to Coetzee's personal life and to the political moment. If these are not always directly articulated, that is partly because of the relentlessly anti-sentimental astringency sometimes verging on cruelty that has remained a hallmark of Coetzee's writing. His marked aversion to gushing in life or literature has manifested itself in a palpable exercise of terse, stoic control. Coetzee's unyielding authorial persona has prompted some, including Nadine Gordimer, to characterize him as a "cold" or "inhuman" writer. It would be no extreme paradox, however, to suggest that almost the opposite is true. At least as regards Coetzee's writing, Hedley Twidle noted that at a time when South African writing was expected to be politically "hot," "Coetzee lowered the temperature . . . until it began to burn, like the strand of a metal fence gripped in winter" (loc. 47). Twidle is not the only Coetzee critic who has resorted to paradox and figurative language, or to contrasts between surface and depth, to convey that the nature and power of Coetzee's writing are not necessarily coextensive with the prose "surface." To take it simply at face value, then, as (again) many have done, is to misapprehend it and offer little basis for the books' extraordinary impact on a global readership.

The "trauma" of the early 1970s included many components overtly present in *Dusklands*. These notably include the shock produced by America's exorbitantly violent, aggressive, and finally unavailing conduct of the Vietnam War, with its disruptive and disillusioning spill-over into American life. The Cold War scenario of anti-Communist American intervention seemed increasingly misplaced. This ideological failure leaves Eugene Dawn, along with an increasing number of Americans, in quest both of another rationale and an effective technology of domination, supplementing military power, to which the resources of social anthropology and media manipulation are harnessed (Noam Chomsky's academic New Mandarins). Such is the mandate Eugene Dawn seeks to fulfill through the practice of what might be called applied mythography, to which his supervisor Coetzee allows a certain scope. The Vietnamese are to be won over and undone through mastery of the mythologies that govern their psychic life—a fantasy akin to that of killing with invisible bullets—while the applied mythographer (one who might now be called an "action intellectual") emerges as the Savior in his own mind. This megalomania may indeed be a symptom of the isolated subject's powerlessness, social alienation, and paranoia, but the grand Vietnam Project focuses on a Vietnam reduced to a dossier of obscene photographs, on which Eugene Dawn dwells with voyeuristic compulsiveness. The "Vietnam War" is hardly more than a composite of fascinatingly horrific images, a pornography of violence.

All this is overt, as is the racialized violence and "megalomania" of the great African adventure, but what is implied in both narratives of *Dusklands* is a shattering of naïve illusions, both public and personal, regarding the white American and South African past. That entails not only disillusionment but also the practically forced acquisition of a new sophistication, widely embraced as a resource of mastery in academic and social life in the early 1970s. The Derridean "always already" was often yoked to this sophistication: one always knew it before it happened; one could never be disconcerted or caught off guard. The shaming of naiveté became the widespread counterpart to this sophisticated posture. As far as I am aware, this often precipitately claimed sophistication passed virtually unquestioned then and later, becoming a "value" in itself. *Dusklands* evinces this sophistication at every level, but also calls its bluff, so to speak.

It is clear in retrospect that *Dusklands* launched what would surely become the most ambitious and consequential metafictional project of our time.[22] Yet Coetzee's metafictional self-consciousness led him on occasion to express envy for great fictional prodigies who seemed to come by it naturally, and whose work is characterized by irrepressible abundance, playfulness, vitality, invention, and humor, without excessive second-guessing. Such a writer he evidently did not consider himself to be. Although he did not say so, I believe his admiration for Defoe implied that Defoe was one of these writers. Dickens too exemplified this enviable condition for him, as may Gabriel Garcia Marquez in *One Hundred Years of Solitude*.

NOTES

1. L.C Knights, "How Many Children Had Lady Macbeth? An Essay In the Theory and Practice of Shakespeare Criticism," *Explorations: Essays in Criticism, Mainly in the Literature of the Seventeenth Century* (London: Chatto & Windus, 1946), 15–44.

2. L.C. Knights, *Drama and Society in the Age of Jonson* (Harmondsworth: Penguin, 1962).

3. Knights sadly recalled having been in the Cambridge University Library when Q.D. Leavis walked in and, pointing at him with a trembling finger, accosted him with the words: "Aha, Professor Judas!"

4. For example, "Triangular Structures of Desire in Advertising," *Doubling the Point: Essays and Interviews* (Cambridge: Harvard University Press, 1992), 127–38.

5. See Bruce Jackson, "Buffalo English: Literary Glory Days at UB," *Buffalo Beat*, 26 (1999). Having so far failed to track down a paper copy of this journal, I can supply only this URL: http://www.acsu.buffalo.edu/~bjackson/englishdept.htm

6. R.G. Howarth, *Two Elizabethan Writers of Fiction: Thomas Nashe and Thomas Deloney* (Cape Town: University of Cape Town Press, 1956); *Minor Poets of the 17th Century* (London: J. M. Dent & Sons, 1931); *Literature of the Theatre, Marlowe to Shirley* (Sydney: Halstead Press, 1953).

7. Trevor Whittock, *A Reading of the Canterbury Tales* (Cambridge: Cambridge University Press, 1968).

8. Patrick Hayes, *J.M Coetzee and the Novel: Writing and Politics after Beckett* (New York: Oxford University Press, 2010), 8.

9. J.M Coetzee, "Isaac Newton and the Ideal of a Transparent Scientific Language," *Doubling the Point*, 184–92; "Simple Language," *White Writing*, 126–29.

10. Wilma Stockenstström, *The Expedition to the Baobab Tree*, trans. J.M. Coetzee (London: Faber and Faber, 1983).

11. On the complex question of Coetzee's relation to Afrikaans, and uses of it, see Rita Barnard, "Coetzee in/and Afrikaans," *Journal of Literary Studies* (2009); Wittenberg, "The Taint of the Censor": 133–150. See also *Boyhood*: 125–27. The Afrikaans dialogues in n the first, South African, edition of *In the Heart of the Country*, suggest that the language provided Coetzee with a linguistic register English did not. In Magda's excruciated addresses to Hendrik, it is as if Afrikaans becomes the medium of extreme role-reversal and breakdown of decorum.

12. The choice between writing in English or one of the African vernaculars has been difficult for black South African writers at all times. Overwhelmingly, those writers have chosen to write in English. None, as far as I know, has followed Ngugi wa Thiong'o's lead in renouncing the English in which his writing career began. One telling exception is the poet Mazisi Kunene who wrote *Emperor Shaka the Great: A Zulu Epic* (London: Heinemann, 1979) in isi-Zulu, but could get the book published only in English translation. In contemporary fiction written by black South Africans, the loss of native fluency among the younger people, along with the loss of a distinctively African cultural heritage, is increasingly registered with alarm. For a growing number of young black people, English is the first and only language.

13. Perhaps a similar impulse animates the Afrikaans poet Antjie Krog, for whom Coetzee has expressed admiration, in her archivally-based "retrieval" of nineteenth century San poems, *The Stars Say 'Tsau': /Xam Poetry of Dia!kwain, Kweiten-ta-//ken, /A!kunta, Han#kass'o, and // Kabbo* (Cape Town: Kwela Books, 2004). A distinguished poetic predecessor in the enterprise of composing "Bushman" poetry in Afrikaans was Eugene. N. Marais (1871–1936), also recalled in *Summertime*.

14. For me, being colonial did not just mean being abjected by people from England but being trapped in the wrong place and time. I found this predicament exemplified by the South African playwright, H.W.D. Manson, who was also a friend. The author of ten now largely forgotten poetic dramas, Manson was isolated from any contact with current world theater or dramatic practice. Despite having a larger than life personality and abundant humor, his dramatic diction was characterized by excruciating "literary" ambition, and dedication to an idea of the heroic polemically opposed to the supposedly anti-heroic ethos of contemporary playwriting, exemplified for him mainly by the work of Samuel Beckett and Harold Pinter. Infused with colonial *ressentiment*, his one comedy, *Potluck*, gleefully fantasized the inundation of contemporary Welfare State Britain. On the one occasion I mentioned him to Coetzee, he remarked only that Manson's sentences seemed singularly elementary.

15. J.M Coetzee, "Samuel Beckett's 'Lessness': An Exercise in Decomposition," *Computers and the Humanities*, 7, 4 (1973), 195–98.

16. *Contrast*. 9.2 (1974), 90–95.

17. William Burchell, *Travels in the Interior of Southern Africa* (1822, 1824), (repr. Cape Town: Struik, 1967). See also Engle: 30.

18. Van Riebeeck Society: Africana in the Making, see http://www.vanriebeecksociety.co.za/ publcats.htm.

19. The bibliography of *White Writing* lists a number of travel narratives written by European visitors to the Cape from the seventeenth through the nineteenth centuries. It should be recalled that observation of the natives of the Cape did not being with the founding of the Cape settlement by Jan van Riebeeck in 1652, but for over a century before that.

20. J.M Coetzee, *Dusklands* (New York: Vintage, 2004): 66.

21. Twidle complains, in *Getting Past Coetzee* (Vintage Digital, 2013), that Coetzee's books are "too teachable," having so fully anticipated their own academic assimilation. For him, that might be a reason to stop teaching them.

22. See, notably, Attwell, *J.M. Coetzee: South Africa and the Politics of Writing*.

Chapter Three

Flashbacks

I have titled this chapter "Flashbacks" partly because it presents no continuous narrative but rather a set of images and recollections remaining from my forty-year friendship with Coetzee, but also going back to childhood in both his case and mine. They are flashbacks to various people and places almost up to the present, but mostly ones centered, as I have already indicated, on the years 1972–74 in Cape Town and its peninsular environs. I will begin, however, with a vivid image that is not my own but one taken from a poem by Anne Carson, titled "Gnosticism IV" and published in *The New Yorker*.[1] It is an image that captures the Coetzee of much gossip and legend, and one to which I can attest:

> ... Coetzee basking
> icily across from you at the faculty table is all at once
> there like a fox in a glare, asking
> And what are your interests?
> his face a glass that has shattered but not yet fallen.

Such is the legendary Coetzee of dinner parties and receptions, an intimidating, frozen, passive-aggressive figure speaking with strained formality if at all and making everyone uncomfortable. (I will suggest later that "What are your interests?" may be a more loaded question than it initially seems.) Commenting on the poem to an interviewer in *The Guardian*, Carson added: "Yes. That was unkind of me, but it's him. I met him once and I can't say he was unkind to me, he was very courtly, but his effect in general was odd. He was confrontationally aloof, if that's possible."[2]

This Coetzee would never be the life and soul of any party. According to one anecdote, at a banquet thrown in his honor by the Irish head of state, various efforts were made to draw Coetzee out, but in the end those present gave up and partied among themselves. Too many people recognize the forbidding dinner guest for the legend to be baseless. Coetzee's vegetarianism, non-consumption of alcohol, and strenuous dedication to cycling make him, in widespread opinion, an ascetic St. John shunning the pleasures and interactions of ordinary mortals. Ironic consciousness of this legendary persona informs *Summertime*, where, to the disapproval of his Afrikaner farm relatives, John passes over the mutton at the evening meal. Although he denies being a "strict" vegetarian, cousin Carol doesn't let his abstention from the sacred mutton of Karroo gastronomy pass without comment, after which "everyone is . . . staring at him. He has begun to blush." He "spears a green bean" (94).

In his biography, Kannemeyer takes up the question of the socially withdrawn, enigmatically silent, even "inhuman," Coetzee, citing contradictory testimony from Coetzee's erstwhile student friends and others showing that, in congenial company, Coetzee can be genial, witty, relaxed, approachable—and a good cook to boot. To that contradiction I can also attest. A gap nevertheless remains apparent between the unbending, distant persona and the relaxed, sociable one. Without purporting to close this gap, I will suggest that it attests to, among other things, Coetzee's pained self-consciousness and lifelong experience of being of being uncomfortably situated in the world. No doubt the origins of that discomfort—not without an element of mortification—are partly situated in the childhood Coetzee recalls in *Boyhood* and *Youth*. Yet I believe the adult discomfort also comprises a quiet detestation of what I can only call inauthenticity in social and intellectual relations. This is not to revive discredited critiques of inauthenticity, but rather to credit a certain easily incensed ethical fastidiousness in Coetzee's relation to the world. It should be added that Coetzee's extraordinary productive achievement implies constant inward preoccupation and detachment from distracting or debilitating public circulation.

In Cape Town, despite a certain abstemiousness and reticence, Coetzee frequently socialized both as a host and a guest. It was during this time that my former spouse, Katherine, and I socialized on many occasions with John and his wife Philippa, one regular haunt being the Indian restaurant Takari in Claremont. Coetzee attended our dinner parties and those thrown by others on Cape Town's almost too active dinner-party circuit. Cape Town colleagues Coetzee found congenial included Philip Birkinshaw and Cathy Salomon, owners of an attractive beach house at Blouberg with the magnificent, "classic" view of Table Mountain ("classic" houses and lifestyles went a long way towards defining the white South African good life in the Western Cape). Coetzee's slightly edgy friendship with the poet-academic Daniel Hutchinson went back to their student days at UCT. Non-academic friends included Chris and Helene Perold. The principle seemed to be that people who were neither tense in Coetzee's presence nor overawed by his intellect and persona could in fact draw him out. Birkinshaw was certainly one of these: handsome, worldly, easygoing, and hospitable, he enjoyed his own celebrity as a Shakespearean actor and was too far removed intellectually from Coetzee to feel any threat from him. Another principle seemed to be that Coetzee found it easier to engage with smart, articulate women who were not overawed by him than with men: these included his current partner, Dorothy Driver, and my own partner Melissa Zeiger. (Years later, at a party at our house in Norwich, VT, Coetzee hugged and kissed Melissa in greeting. One of his former Cape Town graduate students, looking on, said "I almost fell down stone dead.")

Katherine and I socialized frequently at home with John and Philippa, while our son James played with their children Nicolas and Gisela (James and Gisela then being about five). Yet couples socializing at either of our homes brought out a certain underlying malaise in their lives and in our own. These encounters devolved repeatedly into playing charades, on which they more than we insisted. These games were understood to be a more entertaining way of bonding and passing the time than engaging in academic chitchat and malicious gossip (not that Coetzee or his wife were wholly averse to these), the primary currencies of Cape Town social life. Passing the time often felt, however, like killing time while waiting for something to happen. A social life without content—or with undercurrents that would later come to the surface—seemed to be the unacknowledged reality with which we were contending.

At one level, that may have been part of a South African condition to which Coetzee alludes in *Summertime:* "Our attitude was that, to put it briefly, our presence [in South Africa] was legal but illegitimate. We had an abstract right to be there, a birthright, but the basis of that right was fraudulent . . . we thought of ourselves as sojourners, temporary residents, and to that extent without a home, a homeland" (210). An underlying sense of illegitimacy gave a certain tenuousness and vacuity to social existence; it was a matter of waiting for the inevitable cataclysm or moving elsewhere.

In the case of John and Philippa, this sense of not being at home in South Africa was clearly heightened by their uprooting from the United States. To a degree, that uprooting was offset for both of them by the ravishing beauty, congeniality, and familiarity of Cape Town, the Cape Peninsula, and adjacent areas like the Cedarberg. These offered unlimited sightseeing, walking and cycling, while swimming beaches were available on all sides, as was the delightful Kalk Bay fishing harbor, at which fish could be bought straight off the boat. Yet the pleasures of the Cape did not necessarily suffice to stave off depression. Whatever the stresses of Vietnam-era American life, and however unappealing the city of Buffalo may have been, they offered a singularly rich and varied cultural milieu in which the Coetzees had made friends. To my perception, Coetzee never evinced the slightest interest in mingling with Cape Town's arty, affluent, élite.

In Cape Town, the Coetzees tried to retrieve some of what they had lost. They liked to invite students more than they did colleagues. The inexpensive, seemingly haphazard, décor of their house spoke of the American academic counterculture rather than bourgeois Cape Town. Pot-smoke and incense sometimes wafted around. Indian music (Ravi Shankar) or current avant-garde compositions would be played at Coetzee parties. It was there that I first heard the music of the Greek composer Mikis Theodorakis, a now somewhat eclipsed idol of the Left, but then on the cutting edge as well as being a favorite of Philippa, immersed in the study of modern Greek. It was chez Coetzee that I first heard The Band.

As he indicated in *Youth*, Coetzee had highly developed musical taste, attempted to play the piano, and even nourished some musical ambitions. David Lurie's attempt to compose an opera on Byron in *Disgrace* attests to that history. So does the opera based on his novel *Slow Man*, premiered in Poznan, Poland, in 2012, for which Coetzee wrote the libretto while Nicholas Lens composed the music (they are reportedly working on another opera.)[3] The power of Bach's music is a recurrent topic in Coetzee's fiction;[4] at the other end of the musical spectrum, he was drawn to twentieth century atonal avant-gardism, part of the reason being that he perceived the importance of silence rather than sound in some of these compositions. More precisely, Coetzee believed that sound could be used to trace the contours of unfathomed silence rather than break it. Coetzee was certainly impatient with concert hall repetition of the same old repertoire, and preferred even imperfectly executed live performance to canned LP renditions. In an interview with Rian Malan, he responded to a question about what music he liked by saying that he liked music he hadn't heard before.

Coetzee took film-going seriously, although not only in art houses. The cavernous mainstream cinema in Plumstead offered the current fare. To me, if not to Coetzee, even the mainstream films revealed innovation in American filmmaking. One of these films was Stanley Kubrick's *2001: A Space Odyssey*, which seemed philosophically deep and challenging as well as spectacular at the time. On a lower level, *Electra Glide in Blue*, with Robert Blake, seemed both puzzling and absurd, but evidently not to Coetzee, in its fetishization of the Harley. These films were a disorienting departure from black and white film society fare, marked by annual returns of Bergman's *Wild Strawberries*. American pop culture was evidently becoming high. No coherent picture had yet taken shape, even though films like *Midnight Cowboy* and *Easy Rider* had seemed to herald a new type of Hollywood film as early as 1969.

At the same time, however, art-house film making seemed increasingly cognizant of the cultural impact of popular film, as in Victor Erice's *The*

Spirit of the Beehive (El espíritu de la colmena) (1973), with its vivid recall of James Whale's *Frankenstein*, on which Coetzee seized when it came along. Neither of us, I believe, was in a position to grasp fully the post-Civil War import, including the silent interplay of adult and child consciousness, of the film in Spain, nor, of course, could we know that the film would become a landmark in modern Spanish filmmaking.

I do not recall that Coetzee had any particularly strong interest in painting or visual culture—he seemed very much a creature of the word—but I do recall a moment in which I said that one of my relatively few experiences of artistic sublimity occurred in the Mark Rothko exhibition in London's Tate Gallery. An entire room was devoted to a set of large, red and black abstract paintings that individually and collectively, especially collectively, produced an overwhelming impact. Coetzee recalled them in the same way. In *White Writing*, Coetzee revealed his familiarity with the nineteenth century aesthetic discourses of the sublime and the beautiful, and was the first, as far as I am aware, to recognize the shaping power of these discourses—and of landscape painting—on the English poetry written in South Africa during the nineteenth century.

The relatively avant-garde Coetzee household was an attractive space, and their lives were not without bohemian components: for example, they frequented the beautiful, secluded nude beach at Sandy Bay on the Cape peninsula, where Katherine and I had our first experience of a nude beach in their company. Yet, especially for the mercurial Philippa, this all seemed like shadow rather than substance. She clearly mourned the life she had enjoyed in America, and fondly recalled working for the classicist and translator William Arrowsmith. She had begun to study modern Greek in America, and continued to do so, but with failing resolve. Sometimes she blamed the somber John for her predicament, casting herself as Persephone trapped in Pluto's kingdom. In a letter dated 5/17/1990, written to Philippa after the onset of her last illness, my former spouse Katherine wrote appreciatively:

> You probably don't realize how much I have kept thinking about you, and how much my experiences in the States have vindicated your beliefs and attitudes... you were a forerunner of all the qualities I was later to like so much in American women, and a cause for the optimism I now feel about the way things can go for women.

Philippa seemed desperately trapped in Cape Town, and under-employed as an administrative assistant at UCT.

The Coetzee household did not seem happy. The house itself, whether rented or owned I am not sure, would have counted as a shack in the middle class South African reckoning. Admittedly, it was situated in the beautiful suburb of Tokai, a mix of vineyards and upper middle class houses, not a lower middle class dormitory suburb like the Plumstead of Coetzee's *Boyhood*. As noted in *Summertime*, Tokai was also the location of the notorious Polsmoor prison complex to which Nelson Mandela was transferred shortly before his release. The presence of the prison may have been a salutary reminder of the political basis of white privilege, but it was uncomfortably close and intrusive. The Coetzees had acted on a prudential maxim of the impecunious that one chooses either the worst house in a good area or the best house in a bad area. Their choice, the former, was not unreasonable given the incomes of junior academics at the time. Nevertheless, the house was small, damp, draughty and dark, with low ceilings. It was cheerless in the long, wet, Cape winters. Still, it possessed a certain hippie élan alongside its bourgeois neighbors.

John and Philippa seemed deeply bonded yet also temperamentally ill matched, often silently conflicted. Their pathways were also diverging, and it was no surprise when they divorced in 1980 (Philippa died of metastatic breast cancer in 1991.) There were other, unconcealed relationships, and nights spent away from home, especially on Philippa's part. This liberated situation appeared to produce strain. I generally did not pry into Coetzee's relationships, nor was he often disposed to unburden himself. His manner and persona seemed fortified, above all, against intrusion. Despite or because of this fact, he possessed a certain Byronic aura that clearly had its effect. As in *Summertime*, he often extolled the beauty of Cape Town women, and the appreciation was not purely disinterested. In *Disgrace*, he takes his leave of Byronism and romantic passion, self-consciously re-identifying himself with Byron's middle aged, discarded mistress, Teresa, yet that was a later development. In some instances, the woman in question was a student (I should make it clear that I do not regard the Melanie episode in *Disgrace* as autobiographical, any more than I do other specific relationships in Coetzee's fiction.) At that time, codes governing relationships between male faculty members and women students were more permissive than they are now, as long as no unseemly scandal ensued (that tolerance no longer obtains in *Disgrace*). I know that in some of Coetzee's relationships, women became dangerously fixated stalkers, threatening unpleasant consequences. Perhaps that is one of the things that made his "treatment" of women a topic of gossip, but I can pass no judgment. All this seemed to be part of an occasionally turbulent love life that required periodic damage control. I do not believe any of this was particularly secret.

To bring the question of marital relations momentarily closer to home, I shall note that, in his biography of Coetzee, Kannemeyer writes: "On the eve of the publication of *Dusklands* in 1974, John was involved in a triangular relationship with the wife of a colleague. The whole affair is oddly reminiscent of the strange ambivalence of the quartet in Madox Ford's novel *The Good Soldier*, the author Coetzee elected as the subject of his M.A. dissertation. After a phase of near-hypnotic paralysis for all the participants, John's colleague and his wife moved to the US. John was left behind to care for his rabbits, and the husband continued his academic career in the US" (323–24). In the context of Kannemeyer's book, I alone can be this unnamed colleague. No source for the information is given; I can only guess that Coetzee's and my former colleague, Daniel Hutchinson, was the informant since he has alluded elsewhere to this "threesome." Without either confirming or denying this story, I will content myself with saying that Kannemeyer has chosen the wrong novel with the wrong plot.

Kannemeyer begins the story by reporting that "The Coetzees returned from the US with the idea of an open, broad-minded marriage in which both partners could go their individual way, free to pursue other relationships and return to each other when it suited them. Philippa was very open about this with friends like the Perolds" (323). The Coetzees among others were importing the American sexual revolution into a still-provincial white South Africa. The prospect of sexual liberation and of generally more "sophisticated" sexual consciousness and practice certainly sexualized social interaction and placed many conventional marriages under pressure. This new dispensation was distinct from the reputed one of suburban "key parties" and "wife-swapping," both regarded with disdain, yet lights-out dancing and groping became common events. They were not surreptitious; rather, they were taken to manifest openly the newly liberated spirit of things. (Although gay relationships were known and sanctioned, they had not yet fully entered the sphere of "liberation.") Women like Philippa operated confidently as sexual free agents, in the workplace as well as outside it. As a departmental administrative assistant, Philippa may or may not have been involved with the faculty around her, but her overriding interest in their sexual potentialities was undisguised. Things had generally become more fluid and experimental.

Reverting to the Coetzee family scene, Nicolas and Gisela were bright, attractive children. The parents, fond though they were, treated them with the anti-sentimental toughness and irony not infrequently cultivated by educated, middle class parents. Much of the irony went over the children's heads. When things got bad at one time, John took them to a child psychologist. This therapist insisted that the parents come in to participate in family therapy. Coetzee reported with mild chagrin that he had looked forward to a high-level Lacanian exchange with the therapist, but had been given short shrift. Philippa's hippie custom of wandering around the house naked struck the therapist as a problem.

The children were initially sent to the Rudolf Steiner School, a consciously enlightened parental choice against the philistine authoritarianism of both public and private schools of the time, yet the results were mixed. Not only did that schooling not prove academically superior, but it also made the children feel uncomfortably removed from the mainstream. Coetzee's mother, Vera, was clearly troubled about the children, and wished to take them under a more conventional, grandmotherly wing. Whether she was primarily concerned about the "disorderly" regime under which the children were being brought up—disorderly, that is to say, in relation to South African bourgeois norms—or whether she perceived deeper problems I cannot say, since the children's condition was obviously not a topic of discussion outside the family.

The subsequent history of these children was harrowing. Kannemeyer supplies a fairly detailed account. Speaking only on the basis of what I know, suffice to say that Nicolas, having been a sporting star and successful scholar, began to have "problems" in his teens, having "fallen into bad company." There was talk of alcohol, drugs, and petty criminality. He nevertheless enrolled at the University of Cape Town, where one of his English professors, the Shakespearean David Schalkwyk, found him "bright and pleasant." It was during this period of his life that he appears to have developed a very serious problem with alcohol. Hoping that relocation might help, John tried unsuccessfully to enroll him at San Francisco State; at one time, Nicolas worked as a gardener in Golden Gate Park. Finally, however, in 1989, he died by falling out of an apartment window in Johannesburg under circumstances that were never fully clarified. [5] The incompletely processed residue of this calamity appears in Coetzee's *The Master of Petersburg*.[6] Coetzee was teaching in the Johns Hopkins Writing Seminar when he heard the news, and was excruciatingly marooned in Baltimore while waiting for a flight home.

Gisela's life also followed a troubled course. Having been a student at the University of Cape Town and having lived abroad, apparently at Coetzee's expense, she too developed serious problems with alcohol and drugs. She became epileptic, and suffered serious injuries as a result. Severe physical and mental damage eventually required her long-term hospitalization, although with some recent indications of improvement.

Nonstandard parenting, domestic strain, and a divorce may all, obviously, have contributed to the unhappy fate of these children, but so may her mother's death in Gisela's case, and so may any number of imponderables. A punitive, moralistic belief in sole parental responsibility, without regard, for example, to school and social environments or possible genetic idiosyncrasies, might lead to the conclusion that the parents were directly responsible for these children's misfortunes, but then it goes without saying that parallel histories to those of the Coetzee children are legion in families of every kind. I never saw the Coetzees act as anything but responsible, concerned parents, attached to their children and clearly perturbed by their tribulations. John made every effort to bring them back from the brink.

Who knows what positive or adverse effect Coetzee's formidable presence and personality may have had on these children? That it must have had an effect can hardly be doubted; there is no shortage of evidence that it could overpower or intimidate even adults in no familial relation to him. Yet I never heard of any complaint on the children's part that it was hard to live in his orbit. His growing success and recognition could have made them feel that it was impossible to live up to him, and could have made them feel increasingly insecure or inadequate. I have no idea whether, or how, he tried to adjust his family relationships to these changes.

In a letter to me dated 2/12/1983, before the worst had befallen, Coetzee wrote:

> On the domestic front, things are still chugging along. Nicolas still alternates between Philippa's place and mine. I feel that I'm losing touch with them, that I could be doing better. People say I should impose a stricter discipline on them; my feeling is that discipline for its own sake isn't good enough – there's no point in demanding that they spend their free time at home when there is nothing much of interest at home.

Broader family relationships were not untroubled. Coetzee detested his brother in law, Cecil Jubber, for whom Philippa retained a childhood fondness. Jubber was a well-known broadcaster with the SABC, the state broadcasting monopoly, and thus tainted by association with the state radio service. Reputedly an alcoholic, Jubber seemed demoralized, his problems possibly exacerbated by being a gay man in a deeply homophobic culture. Philippa found him embarrassing, but was nevertheless pained by the family estrangement.

In conversation, Coetzee tended to magnify the oedipal drama of his relationships with his own parents, especially his mother. That relationship was subsequently written large in *Boyhood*. It was difficult for me to see in this seemingly ordinary, elderly South African grandmother the looming maternal specter of Coetzee's psychic life. In my own encounters with Coetzee's father, Jack, he too seemed like an ordinary South African man, possessed of a certain bonhomie and a taste for sport. He acted as an umpire in high-level provincial cricket matches. Both *Boyhood* and *Summertime* include excruciated accounts of Coetzee's dealings with his father, an attorney working for the state who was made redundant with the advent of the Afrikaner Nationalist government in 1948, and was later disbarred for trust-fund embezzlement. If this history made it impossible for Jack to assume the awesome stature of the oedipal Father, giver of the Law, in Coetzee's mind, all the more did he remain the deficient father in an exasperatingly failed oedipal scenario. Coetzee's interest in the "father-voice" in "The Vietnam Project" and in the figure of Stalin in Mandelstam's "Stalin Ode" implied a need to imagine the Father in all his sublime horror. Coetzee's accounts of his parents were consistent with a tendency to infuse his personal narrative and, indeed, his personal relations at times, with sadomasochistic melodrama.

The same tendency was apparent in what I came to think of as a genre of Coetzee anecdotes, in which John was the man to whom bad things happened. One of these anecdotes concerned an occasion in Buffalo when he had been renting a house from a black faculty member. The sewage system had been leaking under the house for some time, and eventually Coetzee had to go into the crawl space and clean up. As a white South African, however, he felt unable to report this to the landlord. Another story concerned his having fallen ill in London during winter, and having lain helplessly prostrate—almost as in a Russian movie scene—in a freezing apartment with frost forming on the windows, unable to help himself. Only the wolves were missing in London. Yet another story concerned his having acquired rabbits for his children. They were placed in a bunny-enclosure at the bottom of the garden, where, instead of being adorable, they turned feral and began to cannibalize each other, thereby shocking the children. Another failed venture in bourgeois parenting. In print Coetzee told one story of an admittedly different order. Shortly after his arrival in 1966 at the University of Texas at Austin to begin his Ph.D. program, Charles Whitman opened fire from the campus tower, killing sixteen people and wounding thirty-one.[7] For some time, Coetzee did not know whether Philippa was safe. Relentlessly anti-sentimental, these disaster-stories constructed a doomed persona, but one extracting a certain grim satisfaction from the recital of misfortune.

As fall of 1974 drew closer, I became more preoccupied with the impending move to the United States. There's no question that this was a horrible and stressful time in South Africa, getting worse, with little good in prospect. Up to the very moment of negotiated political transition in 1994, many South African writers like Rian Malan as well as members of the white public could think of South Africa only against the horizon of racial apocalypse.[8] From a certain white liberal standpoint, almost everyone and everything seemed blighted, and a lot of energy went into obsessing unproductively about the racial impasse.[9] An additional incentive was the dearth of opportunity for graduate study in my field in South Africa. In short, it seemed like a good time to leave. The decision to leave was, however, a reckless, naïve one on my part, made in ignorance of how it would feel to be an impecunious immigrant in a foreign country. Coetzee certainly encouraged me to enroll at Berkeley, to which the aura of the 1960s still adhered, and which was an academic powerhouse. I even suspected a certain vicarious participation in my impending departure for an America now closed to him, although of course almost anyone in his right mind would have given me the same advice.

Entering the US for the first time in 1974 produced both more and less culture shock for me than might be supposed. To enter the US then was to enter the academic and political world of *The Vietnam Project*. Although the war was essentially over by 1974, I did, however, experience some of the continuing stresses that I had previously encountered only on paper. On the other hand, geographically and climatically the Bay Area was probably more like Cape Town and its environs than anywhere else in the US. (If anything, the celebrated beauty of the Bay Area was a comedown after Cape Town.) The Californian "good life" was similar enough to that of the Cape to make a fairly easy transition possible. My first bus ride from San Francisco to Berkeley via Oakland did disconcertingly suggest, however, that apartheid had not been left behind. Beyond superficial impressions, much remained for me to learn about American manners, mores, and bureaucratic routines. It would take years before I felt really situated although perhaps never entirely at home.

By the fall of 1974, the Berkeley turmoil of the 1960s and early 70s was essentially over, and the monolithic university administration had taken charge again. Given the university's revolutionary reputation, I was astonished, even coming from Cape Town, by the formality and hierarchical decorum that prevailed in the English Department. Casual dress was far from signifying equality. I experienced a similar shock at my first MLA convention in New York. Professors and graduate student job applicants were turned out, it seemed to me, like corporate managerial aspirants, not academics as I had known them. Part of the reason was, of course, that people were serious about jobs and about their professional standing in a way that would have made little sense in South Africa; in America, terms like "career" and "ambition" were not used only with ironic disdain.

The legendary Berkeley counterculture was in evidence almost exclusively on Telegraph Avenue and on Sproul Plaza; everywhere else, professionalism and bureaucracy reigned. The biggest buildup of Alameda County police I ever saw on campus provided security for a visit by Prince Charles. The new generation of Berkeley undergraduates, whom I later taught in composition classes, generally loathed the remnants of the counterculture as well as the pestering Moonies. Avoiding eye contact seemed like their new rule. In South Africa, much of the teaching had consisted in lecturing to large classes, without student interaction. Charismatic, popular lecturing was accordingly at a premium. In Berkeley, things were different. In one composition class I taught, a faculty member sent to observe gently complained about my pedagogic "arias."

People still arriving in the city of Berkeley with revolutionary hopes generally seemed to be fugitives from the Midwest, with no realistic conception of what awaited them in an increasingly unreceptive city, in which middle class backlash had kicked in. Sporadic, doomed, student and community struggles with the city for control of People's Park seemed like the last flickering of a revolutionary flame. (Years later, returning from Baltimore on a red-eye flight, I saw this heartbreaking poster outside the subway station: "Join Comrade Bob Avakian in People's Park this Sunday to celebrate the 50th anniversary of the Albanian People's Revolution.") As time went on, street people and street life seemed increasingly demoralized, impoverished, and unglamorous.

In 1974, the shelves of used bookstores were still lined with yard upon yard of the collected works of Marx, Engels, Lenin, and Mao, but they seemed to be gathering dust. The adult movie theaters and massage parlors, ostensibly the commercial flowering of the sexual revolution, were dilapidated and clearly on the way out. The English graduate program had even begun to think of imposing time limits on Ph.D. students, many of whose studies had been derailed during the previous decade. I noted that the chairman of the graduate program looked shifty when I asked how long Ph.D. students were typically taking to graduate (an important question for a foreigner in his thirties with a family).

I did not repine at the changes from the Berkeley of the 1960s since I was not there for the revolution. It was not always easy to accept material and social demotion to being a graduate student, albeit one with adequate fellowship support, nor was it easy to adjust to a social and academic milieu different in so many respects from those of Cape Town. Although she had consented to the move, my wife felt violently uprooted and displaced, as did my son James, whose dislocation was shortly compounded by an extremely serious eye injury. Katherine had to endure unemployment and then underemployment for several years before she enrolled in the UC Berkeley program in Landscape Architecture. Although chosen and welcomed, the birth of our daughter in 1980 brought new responsibilities as well as satisfactions into our lives. Yet the adjustments I was personally required to make hardly add up to an "immigrant narrative" since I was still moving within the global sphere of middle class privilege, bringing cultural capital, and had no language problems. Initially, I did not even burn my boats by resigning from the University of Cape Town.

The trials of relocation were compensated to a degree by relative anonymity and invisibility in Berkeley. In England at that time, it was difficult for any white South African to escape interrogation as a putative white racist and possessor of undeserved wealth. Protesting one's relative poverty or opposition to apartheid seemed weakly defensive, especially if one had no particular credentials as a political refugee or activist. Being lectured on the iniquities of apartheid became tiresome, especially in an England that was, at that time, still the largest foreign investor in South Africa. Encountering South African expatriates was often distressing. Many lived in the past, retelling the same stories over and over again. For most of them, the material and social conditions of entry into an English community had turned out to be prohibitive. Living in London generally meant living too far from a tube station to have ready access to the city.

In Berkeley, on the other hand, it was unusual to come across anyone, black or white, who seemed to possess any particular interest in one's South African antecedents. The University of California was so cosmopolitan that variations of foreign origin seemed to have become largely inconsequential. In fact, no one seemed particularly interested in hearing about anyone's different national histories, political systems, or exotic customs; there were just too many of these. The question "What are you working on?" almost always took precedence. As often as not, black people in stores, enquiring about my accent, said they would love to visit "Africa," "South" entirely failing to register.

What I soon found myself working on was Renaissance literature, consciously because of the distinction of the faculty in that field: Jonas Barish, Stephen Booth, Paul Alpers, and the rising star Stephen Greenblatt, who became my Ph.D. director. (Sadly, Stephen Orgel and Stanley Fish had recently left Berkeley, but I had the good fortune to catch up with them as colleagues years later in the Johns Hopkins English Department.) That field was far removed from South African literature—this was before postcolonial studies—and that may well have been the semi-conscious point. The chance to leave behind an unmanageable history and social situation had presented itself. Immersion in the program placed South Africa at an increasing remove (this book constitutes a modest, belated rapprochement). Yet in hindsight it strikes me that some things carried over.

My review of Coetzee's *Dusklands* represented a breakthrough for me that, in all likelihood, led to my choice of Thomas Nashe as a dissertation topic and subsequent book topic: *The Unfortunate Traveler* was conspicuously the most "postmodern" work of Elizabethan prose fiction.[10] In a letter dated 2/12/83, Coetzee wrote:

> Quite aside from what you say directly about Nashe—where I don't really know enough to know how far you are over the current frontiers of debate—there seems to me to be a number of hints you drop for avenues that could be opened up.

If that was the case, I had unwittingly taken my cue from *Dusklands*.

For several months after I had moved to Berkeley, I wrote letters to maintain the live connection with Coetzee, and also because I felt isolated, disoriented, and deprived of a familiar framework. I appreciated Coetzee's regular, sympathetic replies as well as his knowledgeable comments on the world I had entered. One feature of that world on which I wanted to compare notes with him was that English studies at the graduate level seemed to me curiously disconnected from the Anglocentric gentility and social cultivation that had been part of the package in South Africa. One part of the package that incensed Coetzee was the Cape Town faculty habit of sniggering at the "bizarre," non-English names of students of east-European or non-European origin (by which I do not imply antisemitism). In the immigrant-heavy United States, those names would not have raised an eyebrow. In America, "English" as a discipline had been effectively disconnected from cultural Englishness, and also from the social manners, including endless literary allusion as an exclusive code, that had marked English department life in South Africa. It did, however, take me a while to understand that people could be really good at English studies without the expected accompaniments; the gentry fiction of academic English studies had ceased to obtain in fact.

I believe that both Coetzee and I realized before too long—he sooner than I—that that our correspondence could not really bridge the gap of separation, and neither of us was cut out for flowing, vivid epistolary exchange. Little had I ever reflected on the practiced, conventionalized character of prolific correspondence, a point Coetzee may obliquely have been making in one letter in which he remarked that this was hardly a Byronic exchange. His own letters were "in character" in the sense of being laconic and somewhat withdrawn; what else had I expected?

In the years after 1974, I periodically revisited Cape Town while Coetzee periodically visited the United States, where he had recurring contracts with the Johns Hopkins Writing Seminars, directed by John Barth, and the Committee for Social Thought at the University of Chicago. In 1975, quite shortly after I had left, Coetzee made a business visit to Berkeley, and stayed as our guest in the Spartan graduate student apartment (former military housing built on landfill) in which my family and I lived in Albany. This was hardly the Bay Area of the publicity brochures, or one calculated to impress the visitor. In addition to showing Coetzee the sights, sampling some of the restaurants, and throwing a party at which we introduced him to new friends and colleagues, I engaged in ongoing discussion with him about new trends in theory and criticism. *The Structuralist Controversy* had appeared in 1972, at a time when the Johns Hopkins Humanities Center functioned as the main gateway through which French theory entered the US academy.[11] This volume included Jacques Derrida's "Structure, Sign, and Play," heralding the entry of deconstruction into the Anglophone academy.[12] That wedge essay would be followed by the translation of Derrida's *Of Grammatology* in 1976,[13] and in due course there would be a School of Criticism and Theory, a Yale School, and a general theory-revolution in the academy. In its first incarnation, The School of Criticism and Theory offered mid-career retraining to more traditionally schooled academics, while many older faculty members (resentfully) felt de-skilled and superseded. Both Coetzee and I lived through this history, he having already been exposed to new trends while at Buffalo, but now, three years after our arrival in Cape Town, the landscape had changed dramatically, with structural linguistics—and even the fad for linguistics itself—having been eclipsed by post-structuralism. Exciting as these changes undoubtedly were, it was not easy to find a footing in the rapidly shifting currents of the time: our conversations were part of an effort to do so. I have already said that I do not think Coetzee ever found deconstruction particularly congenial, but he was bound to confront it, along with the work of Foucault, as the shaping forces in current criticism.

On one of my early returns to Cape Town, I visited Coetzee in the house he had acquired in Rondebosch. The Tokai house had been vacated following his separation from Philippa. The new house struck me, in contrast to the hippie Tokai house, as solidly middle class but uncharacteristically gloomy and solitary for that area, with little personal imprint and few creature comforts. I gathered that Coetzee did some of the grim business of caring for his father in this house. Coetzee had picked me up in the Datsun truck that makes an appearance in *Summertime*. It was primitive and austere, unheated and uncomfortable, and looked as if it had been fabricated from sardine cans. That cheap Datsun model may have been a boon to those South Africans who could ill afford motor transport, yet Coetzee was not one of those, and his choice of the vehicle seemed perversely self-mortifying.

It was with relief, then, that I met Coetzee's new partner, Dorothy Driver. At that time, she was a feminist professor of English literature at the University of Cape Town, confident, attractive, spirited, friendly, and self-possessed. She was her own person. The encounter I recall best took place in a restaurant in Rondebosch. Coetzee had been discussing his latest round of problems with Nicolas. Dorothy gently tried to redirect the discussion by casting Nicolas as someone crying out for personal attention and validation. She was not trying to minimize the problems, but could also empathize with Nicolas in a way Coetzee, at that stage, found difficult; the problems had been too numerous and too intractable.

Coetzee became a recurrent visitor to the Johns Hopkins Writing Seminars during and after the time I taught in the Johns Hopkins English Department. John Barth, whom he had met in Buffalo, then headed the Seminars. These visits allowed us to renew live contact, but in certain ways they brought home to us that our paths had diverged. I recall a conversation in the student cafeteria, for example, about literary pastoral. I believe Coetzee must have been working on *White Writing* or *The Life and Times of Michel K*, in both of which questions of pastoral arise. I was eager to acquaint him with current New Historicist studies of Renaissance pastoral, with Louis Adrian Montrose taking the lead, but realized that he wasn't buying. I should have guessed that the densely coded political allegory of early modern English pastoral would be remote from Coetzee's critical interests. Reasons why it was so became fully apparent with the publication of *White Writing* in 1988, in which broader questions are addressed, often in a post-Romantic context, about visual and verbal representations of landscape and their ideological purposes.

On one occasion Coetzee gave a public reading for the Writing Seminars. I believe the excerpt must have been from *The Life and Times of Michael K*. Things went smoothly until question time. After a few desultory questions had been asked and answered, a young black student stood up. It was clear almost as soon as he began to speak that he came from South Africa. After saying something to the effect that Coetzee's writing was all very well, the student then asked whether it would be more appropriate for Coetzee to commit himself to the struggle than to play literary games (that was the tenor of the question). Instead of attempting an answer, Coetzee stood silently facing the student, saying nothing. After tense minutes had dragged on, Barth intervened as chair to end the reading. Had Coetzee really frozen? Was he pointedly refusing to entertain the question, or accept its terms? Snubbing the student? The painful scene seemed emblematic of that particular moment in Coetzee's career as a writer from South Africa, although it was clearly a scene from another planet to Barth and the Writing Seminars audience.

Coetzee visited all the campuses at which I taught, sometimes at my invitation and sometimes not. He visited Tulsa, and Dartmouth three times. On one of the Dartmouth occasions, Coetzee gave a reading from *Boyhood*. I had already read the book and found it grim, as many have done. At the reading, he extracted from the book a dark humor I had not sufficiently appreciated in his work. His reading style was anti-theatrical, austere and subdued. He nevertheless conveyed a strong presence and his subtly inflected reading animated the chosen passages. He was thus a "good reader." He also visited a Dartmouth creative writing class, and nonplussed the professor who had invited him by announcing that he would answer no questions about himself or his writing.

Coetzee's power as a reader of his own fiction manifested itself fully when he gave a reading, to a spellbound audience, as a keynote speaker at an inaugural conference I organized in 2000 as the first director of the newly founded Leslie Center for the Humanities at Dartmouth.[14] The founding of this center implied a continuing dedication on the part of the college both to the humanities and to the liberal education. Yet the title of the conference, "The Future of the Humanities," revealed a concern that has only become more acute about the viability of the traditional humanities education in the contemporary university and in the public domain. Conferences on "the future of the humanities" have proliferated, prompting uneasy recall of the critic Barbara Johnson's dictum that as soon as futures come under discussion, savvy investors bail out. In any event, this conference was meant to reaffirm the value and continuing mutation of the humanities as vital enterprise.

For his keynote address, Coetzee chose to read the graduation speech delivered in the novel *Elizabeth Costello* by Sister Bridget of Marianhill Hospital in Kwazulu-Natal, an institution especially dedicated to the care of AIDS-infected children. The point of Bridget's speech was that the humanities as conventionally understood have no future in Africa, and perhaps little in the world since, according to her, the humanities parted company with their founding rationale at quite an early stage in their history. In her account, the humanism that began as a philological endeavor focused on biblical editing and interpretation in the early modern period declined into secular classical studies supported by academic practices of editing and criticism. These debilitated humanities cannot take root in Africa, let alone minister to the needs of the population. Bridget preempts the argument that the humanities—*litterae humaniores*—have been an enlightened neoclassical enterprise from the start rather than a handmaid of Christian proselytizing. She asserts that the modern humanists "picked the wrong Greeks" in pursuing the idealizing strain rather than the dark, passionate Dionysian one in the Greek world; accordingly, the humanities fail to excite and galvanize those to whom they are presented. As a proffered alternative to religious belief, the humanities possess little traction.

Bridget speaks from the position of a Catholic believer in an overt and implied dialogue with her secular sister Elizabeth, a novelist in the humanistic tradition. The aftermath of Bridget's address is a brilliantly staged debate between her, her academic hosts, and, above all, her sister Elizabeth. Bridget introduces Elizabeth to a black sculptor, Jacob, who has spent his life producing nothing but iterations the same image of the crucified Christ. Bridget proclaims *this* religious art—or craft, since the question of art is moot in this context—authentic. By this she does not mean that Jacob's work possesses an indigenous African authenticity. (The image is obviously derived from Christian iconography of the crucifixion.) Jacob himself dismisses African pictures and masks as purely tourist commodities, in which he has no interest. Authenticity inheres, rather, in Jacob's consuming dedication to the figure of the suffering Christ, not rendered in any naturalistic detail but simply a flat image of suffering. It is also to that figure, speaking to and for them, that members of the community, especially women, can become attached. Such is the anti-humanist art that Bridget holds up as exemplary.

Whatever the force of Sister Bridget's speech in the context of the novel, one could not miss the implied challenge and salutary intent of a speech proclaiming "no future" in the context of a conference dedicated to the projection of a bright future for the humanities. Varied and often interesting though the other conference presentations were, none took up any real challenges to the humanities or proceeded at the high level of the sisters' debate. It can be said that Sister Bridget's history of the humanities is tendentious. Speakers in the novel question it, and indeed the person introducing Coetzee at the conference, Amy Hollywood, now of the Harvard Divinity School, politely challenged Coetzee, in conversation after the talk, on the substance of Sister Bridget's historical account of the humanities. (Coetzee responded only by saying she should complain to Sister Bridget.)

Coetzee's reading was not only provocative in context but intriguingly layered and multidimensional. Aside from the double context of Sister Bridget's address—in the novel, and in a future-of-the-humanities conference—the speech itself was a fictionalized instance of formal public address, a genre Coetzee has practiced on such momentous occasions as acceptance of the Nobel Prize and acceptance of the Jerusalem Prize in Israel. In Coetzee's public reading, the fictional Bridget Costello merged with Coetzee's *propria persona*, making the address a subtly double-voiced utterance, and, in a sense, a self-parody. Coetzee's *propria persona* on this occasion was not, however, that of the public speaker, but rather of the novelist-academic—"the humanities" incarnate, so to speak—whose mere presence no less than his topic posed questions, wholly unaddressed by the conference speakers, regarding the scope and meaning of the humanities in the new millennium. The same could be said in the case of the other keynote speaker, Samuel Delaney, whose encounter with Coetzee was marked by goodwill and fundamental bafflement on both sides.

This was Coetzee's last visit to a campus on which I was teaching. By email, I congratulated him on the Nobel Prize, to which he responded in a message dated May 1st, 2005: "I don't think the Nobel lecture is anything much, but at least it isn't a Pronouncement, which I think most Nobel lectures tend to become." When, under the Bush administration, Dartmouth invited him as a Montgomery Fellow for a term, he declined on the grounds that Bush-era American practices of torture made it unthinkable for him to enter the country. Coetzee had placed torture squarely on the agenda as early as 1982 in *Waiting for the Barbarians*. He had done so in the prevailing South African context of censorship and torture, at the beginning of the 1980s, during which decade and the following one torture, murder, and illegal detention became increasingly the dominant, pervasive governmental exercises of power. (That history was finally exposed through the proceedings of the Truth and Reconciliation Commission.) Coetzee's representation of torture was, in effect, a pointed challenge to the South African censors. As previously remarked, Wittenberg, "Taint of the Censor," notes that both Coetzee and his publishers expected *In the Heart of the Country* to be banned in South Africa on account of its episodes of interracial sex. An inside informant let it be known, however, that the focus of censorship had shifted:

> [The novelist and editor Elsa] Joubert's source was impeccable: her husband sat on one of the censorship committees. The censors, he confided after reading the manuscript, were not any longer concerned about indecency but "at-

tacks on police torture etc. . . . are the current no-no" (19 July 1977). Interestingly, Coetzee's next novel, *Waiting for the Barbarians* (1980) would tackle precisely this theme, though its allegorical framing shielded it from censorship (143).

Allegorical "shielding" from South African censorship was not the only purpose of Coetzee's representation of torture as a device of unspecified "empire." His refusal to localize torture as a purely South African abomination of the apartheid era meant that torture would not simply disappear with the termination of that regime; if the novel is prescient, it is partly so for that reason. Nevertheless, Coetzee wanted his books sold and read in South Africa, and was willing to bargain with the South African censorship up to a point, although Wittenberg does not suggest it ever came to that. If Coetzee "shielded" his representation of torture, there was no guarantee that that shielding would suffice, and he violated precisely the taboo of which his publishers had been informed. Anyone in South Africa could, and most did, see the local point. We are not left to imagine what Coetzee made of the ludicrously denied and simultaneously defended practice of torture under the Bush-Cheney administration.

Coetzee supplied a postscript to this history when I met him at York University, in England, in June 2011, at a Beckett conference at which he gave a remarkable reading from a work in progress, later *The Childhood of Jesus*, to a packed, enthusiastic audience. He told me he had entered the United States again under the Obama administration, but had found himself, on more than one occasion, singled out for special, separate interrogation by the US Immigration Service. When he asked why he was being subjected to this treatment, he was told that he could apply for an explanation under the Freedom of Information Act. At the time we met, he had received no response to his request. He had already bypassed the United States in his most recent travels, and said he intended to continue doing so.

The advent of Elizabeth Costello, an Australian protagonist, evidently coincided with Coetzee's emigration to Adelaide, Australia, in 2002, and assumption of Australian citizenship. This move elicited a certain amount of public and private speculation. His only direct comments to me on the move came in successive emails, the first dated 4/15/2003: "Australia itself is wonderful. It's possible I am badly mistaken, but until I am persuaded so I will continue to believe this is the best move I have ever made." The second, dated 8/5/2007, was less rapturous:

> I was last [in South Africa] in 2005, to receive a state award at the hands of President Mbeki (accompanied by a tight little smile); otherwise, I am trying to make a go of it in Australia, though I know I will never feel other than an outsider here. Dorothy is finding the move harder than I am—she misses her

Cape Town friends . . . but agrees that growing old in South Africa is not a fate to be looked forward to."

In becoming a public critic of the Australian government's participation in Bush-era practices of torture and secret imprisonment, Coetzee made it clear that living in Australia as distinct from South Africa did not mean seeing no evil or succumbing to an escapist utopianism.

NOTES

1. Anne Carson, "Gnosticism IV." *Decreation: Poetry, Essays, Opera* (New York: Alfred A. Knopf, 2005): 90.
2. "Magical Thinking," *Guardian Review*, December 30th, 2006: http://www.guardian.co.uk /books/ 2006/dec/30/featuresreviews.guardianreview
3. See http://bookslive.co.za/blog/2012/07/06/multimedia-slow-man-the-opera-premiers-in-poland-plus-honorary-doctorate-for-coetzee/
4. "Intimate Practices: Music, Sex and the Body in J.M. Coetzee's *Summertime*," forthcoming in *Mosaic* (2016).
5. Kannemeyer, *passim*, extensively documents the histories of Nicolas and Gisela, including the inquest on Nicolas's death.
6. J.M Coetzee, *The Master of Petersburg* (New York: Penguin, 1999). See Derek Attridge, "Expecting the Unexpected: *The Master of Petersburg,*" *J.M. Coetzee and the Ethics of Reading* (Chicago: University of Chicago Press, 2004), 113–37.
7. "Remembering Texas," *Doubling the Point*, 50–53.
8. Rian Malan, *My Traitor's Heart: A South African Exile Returns to Face His Country, His Tribe, and His Conscience* (New York: Atlantic Monthly Press, 1990).
9. Obviously, the situation of black, Colored, and Indian people in this time was, for the most part, immeasurably worse than that of whites, yet paradoxically it may have been less blighted. Many testimonies, including that of Nelson Mandela, exist to the resilient vitality of black township culture in Johannesburg (Alexandra, Orlando, Sophiatown, Soweto). Hugh Masekela, for example, provides a rich account of the irrepressible township musical culture, and particularly of jazz as a medium of political resistance, in *Still Grazing: The Musical Journey of Hugh Masekela* (New York: Three Rivers Press, 2005).
10. Jonathan Crewe, *Unredeemed Rhetoric: Thomas Nashe and the Scandal of Authorship* (Baltimore: The Johns Hopkins University Press, 1982).
11. Richard Macksey (ed.), *The Structuralist Controversy: The Languages of Criticism and the Sciences of Man* (Baltimore: The Johns Hopkins University Press, 1972).
12. Jacques Derrida, "Structure, Sign, and Play in the Discourse of the Human Sciences," tr. Richard Macksey and Eugenio Donato, *The Structuralist Controversy*: 263–64.
13. Jacques Derrida, *Of Grammatology*, tr. Gayatri Chakravorty Spivak (Baltimore: The Johns Hopkins University Press, 1976).
14. On this occasion, I had the foresight to have the talk taped; a DVD remains in the collection of the Jones Media Center at Dartmouth.

Chapter Four

Boyhood

In my preface, I wrote: "On reading *Boyhood*, I think 'Well, at least I won't have to write a boyhood memoir now.' It seems to me that Coetzee has done the job not just for himself but for me as a white, Anglo-South African contemporary sharing the generic experiences of South African boyhood in the 1940s and 50s." By this I do not mean that these generic experiences were identical for all, or that they carried the same subjective import for all those undergoing them. Differences will certainly be evident in the pages that follow. Yet the title *Boyhood* points ambiguously to both the generic and the personal: the boyhood in question is not only that of the individual John Coetzee (or of the artist as boy), or, indeed, of his white South African contemporaries. The abstract condition of "boyhood" can potentially accommodate any reader, not even gender-difference precluding subjective "translation" in the process of reading this fiction. As autobiography in the third person, *Boyhood* does not make the first person J.M. Coetzee its exclusive referent; nobody "owns" this narrative. It is partly for these reasons that I have taken the liberty of including more personal narrative in this chapter than anywhere else in this book.

It obviously remains a question whether the familial and social relations of *Boyhood* actually constitute a portrait of the artist, or account for the writer Coetzee became. The book does help to make intelligible Coetzee's flight to the high ground, so to speak, from the painfully constricted, mortifying conditions of his boyhood. Perhaps the book helps to account as well for the relentless drive that has made Coetzee a prolific and pre-eminent writer of his time, and moreover something of a perfectionist in matters of form and style. Furthermore, *Boyhood* establishes some of the originating conditions of the dissociated, third-person selfhood Coetzee represents as his own, a device that crosses between fiction and autobiography throughout his work.

Yet in a sense the book can do no more than supply data for continuing interpretation. Certainly, to my mind, it supplies no key to unlock the secret of Coetzee's authorship, and I do not believe it is intended to do so.

For one thing, *Boyhood* can be read less as a revealing personal exposure than as Coetzee's contribution to the prolific genre of the boyhood memoir; that is to say, as an exercise in a particular genre that it simultaneously deconstructs. Coetzee makes himself the experimental subject, so to speak, of a book that is not autobiographical, as some early reviewers disapprovingly noted, but is instead a dissociated third-person narrative of "boyhood." If Coetzee thus deconstructs the genre, in the same process he manipulates one of its primary conventions, namely that the protagonist can inhabit the narrative in two different guises, in two widely separated moments of consciousness, one existing in the recollected past and one in the present. Nostalgia, sentimentalization, and narcissism regarding the child self are abiding temptations of the genre, as is the romantic scenario of constructing the child as father to the man. The Coetzee of *Boyhood* could not be more keenly aware of these generic pitfalls, against which he defends sardonically, nor could he be more aware of the fictional character of this or any other self-portrayal. Yet the convention nevertheless yields two selves in *Boyhood*, but ones that become indistinct through the use of the present tense and of free indirect speech: the pronoun "he" can and often does designate both at once. The two figures interpenetrate atemporally even though the narrative registers change and the passing of time. In a sense the title *Boyhood* is therefore ironic: the boy is not confined to boyhood but remains present in the adult's "life in writing."

Admittedly, *Boyhood* does bear the sharp imprint of a particular time and place, recognizable to me as the time and place in which my boyhood story transpired as a parallel and often-overlapping one. Despite the caveat in my preface against making this book "my story and Coetzee's place in it," this chapter will include elements of my story that will, I hope, expand the generic picture of white South African boyhood, mostly in the rural and small-town milieu that constituted South African "provincial life." I shall comment on, and also hope to amplify, the data supplied in *Boyhood*.

For me, the recognizability of *Boyhood* begins with the minute recall of telling detail that makes the book, as an anonymous reviewer quoted on the Penguin book jacket writes, "an uncannily accurate picture of the way things were in South Africa." I could list particulars, on page after page of *Boyhood*, of locales, sights and sounds, objects and commodities, turns of expression, states of mind, relations to others, physical sensations, forms of affective attachment and detachment, that contribute to this "accurate picture." Verifying this accuracy point by point would, however, serve little critical purpose. I can only affirm it, adding that the "uncanniness" of the recall results partly from the present-tense narration that makes the lost world of Coetzee's boyhood available to any reader. Moreover, Coetzee's retentiveness is not just a matter of recalling affectively charged details, but of reanimating a past that survives only in fading memory. "How will he keep them in his head, all the books, all the people, all the stories? And if he does not remember them, who will? (166). The motive in question is akin to the one professed in the exchange between John and Margot in *Summertime*: "You can speak with the dead . . . who otherwise are cast out into everlasting silence." (104). This *cri de coeur* is a rarity in Coetzee's writing, which seldom allows itself this degree of solemnity. Perhaps this awed sense of obligation to recall the past, to give voice to the dead, and to make present in writing what otherwise lives and dies only in individual memory, constitutes one of the most important motives of Coetzee's writing. Fighting what ultimately has to be a losing battle against disappearance and extinction lends urgency to Coetzee's autobiographical writings, with their reanimating deployment of the present tense. Ultimately the reanimated dead include Coetzee himself, writing "posthumously."

Coetzee details some early encounters with writing and its powers, while at the same time mapping the dreary literary terrain of provincial boyhood in South Africa. The reading matter of the time, painfully familiar to those who were there, includes Paul Gallico's *The Snow Goose, Scott of the Antarctic* (author unnamed), the "low" popular magazines *Argosy* and *The Reader's Digest*. The cinematic counterpart to this thin gruel, shown at what continued to be called the "bioscope" in South Africa long after the term had become obsolete elsewhere, included cliffhanger serials and Errol Flynn swashbucklers: the Coetzee of *Boyhood* complains that Flynn "looks just the same whether he is playing Robin Hood or Ali Baba, while in contrast the fact that "the man who plays Tarzan keeps changing" (45) undermines the credibility of the character. Interminable radio serials complete the entertainment picture.

The school curriculum included more edifying fare (chosen *as* edifying by British classicists and imperial educators) in the guise of Greek and Roman heroic tales: Hector and Achilles, Horatius holding the bridge, Mutius Scaevola. Although we were all being educated to be young South Africans, the country having been an independent and assertive member of the Commonwealth, not technically a colony, since 1911, what could be understood only in retrospect was that the educational machine producing us was still one designed to turn out self-sacrificing, minor functionaries of the increasingly virtual Empire. Roman history was a component in that machine.

The tenacity of the British imperial imaginary would now almost defy belief: a teacher of mine in a middle school history class remarked that all historical empires had come to an end, but one could still hope that the British Empire would be the exception. All the incongruities notwithstanding, the British public school program of "character-training" was exported to the colonies and inflicted on boys of various ethnicities, heritages, and social classes. Perhaps it was in the "English" private and public schools that boys were most openly reminded of their place in the imperial scheme of things. Kipling's "Recessional" was repeatedly sung on high "religious" occasions: [1]

> God of our fathers, known of old,
> Lord of the far-flung battle line,
>   Beneath whose awful hand we hold,
>   Dominion over palm and pine.

The not so hidden agenda of this schooling was to cultivate a vocation for governing "lesser breeds without a law" (l. 327).

Kipling's poem "If" adorned schoolroom walls and became the virtually definitive template for manliness:

> If you can fill the unforgiving minute
> With sixty seconds' worth of distance run,
> Yours will be the earth and everything that is in it,
> And, what is more, you'll be a man, my son (578).

Daughters obviously learned their own lessons in submission in segregated girls' schools. The last two lines do, however, enunciate the tacit bargain of empire: sacrifice yourself and you will receive the world in exchange. If the machine failed to produce the desired product in Coetzee's case, it was partly because he absorbed the Roman narratives into his own nascent process of fictional character-building.

Even Boy Scout training, beginning with induction into the Cubs, retained a live connection to Boer War scouting and to Lord Robert Baden-Powell, the British commander who had conducted the defense of Mafeking. Baden-Powell's scouting manuals, initially written for military use, began to be read by boys, and B-P, as he was known, followed up with *Scouting for Boys* in 1908. For younger boys in the Cubs, Kipling's *The Jungle Book* provided a template for secure, familial, socialization under the Law, the child-protagonist Mowgli being adopted as a "cub" into the jungle "family" over which the old, male, wolf Akhela presides. The tutelary and protective figures of the jungle family, both male and female, defend Mowgli against lawless predators including the Bandar Log, the chattering monkeys who abduct him at one point (and who, in critical legend, represent the journalistic class of Kipling's time).

Boyhood induction included playing games essentially reserved for boys. The game that captivated Coetzee was cricket, which he continued to play long into adult life. The writer Coetzee must have known that his tutelary figure, Samuel Beckett, shared his passion for cricket and had, in fact, been a first class player. In the still somewhat bilingual and bicultural milieu of Coetzee's boyhood, cricket playing did not necessarily signify ethnic Englishness, any more than it did elsewhere in the colonies. Coetzee's passion for the game was clearly overdetermined. It constituted a bond between him and his father, Jack. In his exchange with Margot, John alludes to the passion for cricket he shares with his father. As a boyhood activity, the game served as a male refuge from many uncongenial realities, including his difficult relationship with his mother. Yet Coetzee also observes in *Boyhood* (54) that cricket "is the truth of life": on the field, what you are made of cannot be hidden.[2] Despite or because of his postmodern sophistication, here and elsewhere Coetzee designates an ingrained truth finally immune to irony: in this small instance he thus draws a line at the easy irony always at hand in so much postmodern criticism.

Gender training at school included the beginnings of sexual socialization. In *Boyhood*, that process took place largely through the language of apparently more knowing Afrikaner boys, many, no doubt, from farms, with their own set of gross terms for body parts and a lingo in which, for example, a penis was a "piel" and condoms were "effies" (more often than not, boys bandying the term had never laid eyes on a condom). This crude induction had at least two long-term effects, not just on the sensitive, Anglicized Coetzee of *Boyhood*, but on boys acculturated as English: first, fear and shock induced by the perceived crudity of Afrikaner boys, and, second, the erection of a barrier to any comprehension of girls as sexual beings or even as people with whom boys could interact. That situation was greatly exacerbated by attendance at boys' boarding schools that rendered girls alien. In a pathetic attempt to overcome this alienation, schools like the one I attended would hold an annual dance, before which they would bring in professional dance instructors to teach the rudiments of ballroom dancing. The women tasked with instructing clumsy, reluctant teenage boys were certainly earning their keep.

Coetzee's induction into sexual language did not necessarily make the adult, fiction-writing, Coetzee into what he or others would call a feminist. As a writer he has, however, been conspicuous for adopting female personae, or, more accurately, writing from the empathetically imagined positions of women. If there is a sequel to the encounter with Afrikaner boys in *Boyhood*, it appears in *Age of Iron*, where Coetzee's schoolboy recall merges into the consciousness of the English-speaking female protagonist, contemplating TV images of the Afrikaner nationalist rulers of South Africa:

> Television. Why do I watch it? The parade of politicians every evening: I have only to see the heavy, blank faces so familiar since childhood to feel gloom and nausea. The bullies in the last row of school desks, raw-boned, lumpish boys grown up now and promoted to rule the land . . . legitimacy they no

longer trouble to claim. Reason they have shrugged off. What absorbs them is
power and the stupor of power. Eating and talking, munching lives, belching.
Slow, heavy-bellied talk . . . pressing downwards, their power in their weight.
Huge bull testicles pressing down on their wives, their children, pressing the
spark out of them. In their own hearts no spark left. Sluggish hearts, heavy as
blood pudding.[3]

Induction into boyhood at school also included the frequent caning that was so ubiquitous and unchallenged a feature of the British and colonial educational system. If remote, elementary state schools of the kind recalled in *Boyhood* tended to minimize the "higher" promises of Empire—they were, after all, English or dual-medium rather than "English" schools—they certainly did not compromise on the beatings that were a staple of British education. Boys were expected to "take it like a man." This school beating was continuous with the horrific flogging practiced in the colonial penal system, although of course penal flogging, mostly inflicted on men of color, was of a different order from that meted out in schools. Men might emerge from that ordeal literally and figuratively scarred for life. School beatings had always had their perverse as well as brutal aspect: in the well-known case of Algernon Charles Swinburne, being beaten at school evidently instilled a lifelong predilection. The terrorizing abusiveness and traumatic residue of school flogging have, however, become a talking point in recent times. To take one example, controversy flared in England following a review by the politician Paul Foot of Mark Peel's *The Land of Lost Content: The Biography of Anthony Chenevix-Trench*.[4] Omitted from this and other laudatory accounts of Chenevix-Trench, a former headmaster of Shrewsbury and Eton, was his penchant for caning boys on their bare buttocks, with fondling thrown in. Foot claimed that this was an open secret to all who had attended those schools. Following Foot's example, others contributed to the public exposure of abusive flogging.

In *Boyhood*, Coetzee makes no bones about the centrality of beating to the school experience:

> What happens at school is that boys are flogged. Boys are ordered to bend over and touch their toes and are flogged with a cane. (5).

Every teacher at his school, man or woman, has a cane and is at liberty to use it.

What sets Coetzee apart in this milieu his inability to acquiesce in being caned. This is not a matter of principled resistance at that time in his life; in fact, he blames his mother for not having inducted him by beating him, as a normal mother (or real father) would have done. He believes he can overcome his terror of beating by simply getting it over with, yet "he knows he will not be able to endure the shame" (7). This apparently singular susceptibility to shame remains unexplained, but it contributes to Coetzee's representation of a person (a subject) whose singularity remains ultimately unaccountable. This suggestive detail traces the birth of perfectionism to shame-avoidance: the shame-prone John of *Boyhood* must be perfect at all times and give no occasion for beating. Openly resisting would merely pile shame upon shame, setting him apart from all the other boys. Permanent, secret terror thus becomes the condition of school life, the lifelong imprint of which *Boyhood* implies.[5] One of my own science teachers, a school "character" like Coetzee's Mr. Lategan, devoted his entire first lesson to the punishments he would inflict for various offenses in the lab: "I'll hit you hell-hard."

In my more "English" boarding school experience, caning was the prerogative of all teachers, but it was also delegated to senior boys designated "prefects." The teachers, who might be poor disciplinarians who would cane to no avail, relied on these supplementary beatings to maintain discipline. In one school I attended, prefects were allowed to beat boys with the "black snake," a length of rubber hose trimmed down to a point. The punishment was administered with unconcealed relish. In a violent spiral, certain boys would defiantly provoke further punishment. Coetzee writes in *Boyhood*:

> Miss Oosthuizen never succeeds in making Rob Hart cry; perhaps that is why she flies into such rages with him and beats him so hard, harder than anyone else. Rob Hart is the oldest boy in the class . . . he has a sense that between Rob Hart and Miss Oosthuizen there is something going on that he is not privy to. . . . Rob Hart is part of a world he has not yet found a way of entering; a world of sex and beating (6).

That "world of sex and beating" was one in which one might occupy in turn the positions of the beaten or the one beating, thereby passing on the wound. My own change of position came after I had completed my undergraduate degree and was employed as a teacher for one year by my former boarding school. All teachers were expected to inflict corporal punishment for a range of offenses. This was not quite the hysterical free-for-all described in *Boyhood* but a regulated system in which teachers were authorized to administer two strokes on the buttocks with a cane. This punishment was nevertheless no laughing matter. Having fairly recently been on the receiving end, I found it strange and unsettling, to say the least, to be on the giving end, especially after four years spent in a (relatively) liberal, enlightened university milieu. As in *Boyhood,* teachers were expected to acquire their own canes. These had to come from somewhere: a strange tobacconist in a nearby town sold them, presumably catering to a market not wholly confined to novice high school teachers. The source of these canes made all-too-apparent the crossover between school discipline and other forms of "discipline." For me, the contradiction between this "world of sex and beating" and the relatively enlightened one of university liberal education produced is own shame, from which a flight from school teaching after one year provided my release.

As everyone knows, homosexuality among boys was not only a social fact of British boarding school life but also a trope of English fiction in the twentieth century. What went for British public schools certainly went for South African boarding schools. Same-sex relations were punitively stigmatized as well as being against the school rules. While "out" gay relations were impossible, in one school I attended a group of boys defiantly formed what they called "The Knitting Club." Even now, I can only marvel at their insouciant nerve. While some teachers obsessively tried to ferret out offenders, others, probably the majority, knew enough to leave well alone.

For the Coetzee of *Boyhood*, school included not only sex-gender training but identification within the narrow range of options existing within the field of South African whiteness. As we have already seen, the encounter with Afrikaner schoolboys resulted in shocked recoil, a reaction shared, I believe, by most English speaking youth. Both critical reflection and more complex or congenial interactions with adult Afrikaners were needed to undo that aversion. Prejudice against Afrikaners was deep-rooted, as adult Afrikaners well knew; it was a prejudice for which the adult Coetzee had no patience, especially insofar as it entailed ignorant prejudice against the Afrikaans language. Jewishness both did and did not fit in; assimilation and dissociation represented contrasting options for Jewish inhabitants of the country. Moreover, Jewish immigrants entering the country in the early twentieth century were not necessarily "white-identified." Immigrants cohabited, for example, with the "colored" inhabitants of Cape Town's District Six. In the Afrikaner countryside the itinerant pedlar or *smous* was a familiar figure, while city Jews figured in Afrikaner fiction as rapacious bankers and magnates. In the world of *Boyhood*, however, Jews represented a somewhat unknown quantity. It is partly for that reason that the disaffected young John is drawn to them.

In one of the more comical school scenes in *Boyhood*, the protagonist has to choose between identifying himself as a Christian, a Catholic, or a Jew. Jews and Catholics are excluded from Protestant (aka "Christian") school prayers. Perversely, John identifies himself as a Catholic, even though his family has no religion and he knows nothing about Catholicism. (This choice is a counterpart to his secret choice of the Russians over the Americans in the Cold War taking of sides during his boyhood.) The Catholic boys are dubious about his claim, and keep on pressing him about whether he attends Catechism. Even knowing nothing about Catholicism, however, the young John could have been aware of its bogeyman status in rural, Afrikaner, Calvinist South Africa.

Calvinist preachers still routinely inveighed against the "Roomse gevaar" (Roman danger) from the pulpit. Without escaping the apartheid structure,

Catholicism was non-racial in principle, one consequence of which, in my own early convent experience, was that that black and white children would mingle to celebrate Corpus Christi together as equals, an experience available in no other way. The Catholic Church later refused government school-subsidies contingent upon complete segregation.

Catholicism also figured European exoticism and decadence, another potential "danger." My own convent experience had exposed me to palpably alien Europeans in the guise of German Dominican and Irish Loretto nuns, the latter with pointed stories to tell us, as British imperialists in the making, about what their families had endured in Ireland under the licensed terrorism of the English Black and Tans.[6] To encounter Catholicism was also to encounter the whole gaudy paraphernalia of the Latin mass, elaborate vestments, rosaries, incense burners, feast days, Maids of Mary, altar boys, and stained glass: in short everything calculated to outrage a Calvinist sensibility.

The nature of the "Jewish danger" remains largely undefined in *Boyhood* in the absence of a visible Jewish culture in the provinces. (Among the "gevaars" by which Afrikaners thought themselves beset, the "swart gevaar" [black peril] increasingly took precedence.) What motivates the bullying by Afrikaner boys remains opaque, or perhaps the manifestation of the longstanding Protestant anti-Semitism to which Luther had given impetus. At the level of adult rationalization, Jews figured as the dominant force in mining and high finance, at a time before Afrikaners had seriously penetrated that domain. The woes of Afrikaner "poor whites," many of them displaced from the countryside, could readily be laid at the door of the Jews, not "rooted" in the countryside yet determining its fortunes from remote urban locations. Insofar as what remains unspoken in *Boyhood* is infused with the ethos of the *plaasroman*, the stigma attaches to:

> The figure of the monied townsman . . .more often than not Jewish, looking for viable farming operations in which to invest. . .the capitalist is portrayed as a scheming villain (the Jew in *Die meulenaar* whose excuse is that "business is business") (78–9).

Complementarily rather than contradictorily, a number of European Jews had also brought with them forms of European political radicalism, including Communism, that endured at least through the 1960s, contributing to simmering Afrikaner anti-Semitism. One such radical was Wulf Sachs, author of *Black Hamlet*,[7] who had been a disciple of Freud and who opened the first psychoanalytic practice in South Africa, in Johannesburg. Sachs's attempt to open a non-racial office immediately came into conflict with urban segregation and zoning laws. During the 1960s, anti-apartheid activism conspicuously included Jews like Dennis Goldberg, Harold Wolpe, Joe Slovo, Albie Sachs, Ruth First, Arthur Goldreich, and Helen Suzman, a fact not lost on antisemites in the government. In my own generation, two of these activists were David Ernst and Victor Finkelstein, as it happens two of my undergraduate bridge-plying companions. I had no inkling that they were involved in underground activities until I woke one morning to see a newspaper headline announcing their arrest on serious charges. They drew heavy sentences. It later transpired that Ernst's roommate had been informing on him for years.[8]

It is finally to the Jewish boys that the young John of *Boyhood* is most drawn, and with whom he feels most identified. They ask no questions about his religion, and are of the social class in which children always wear shoes. They are brutally persecuted by Afrikaner bullies in the school, for whom the term "Jood"—Jew—is an insult. Coetzee's initial, homoerotically-tinged bonding with Greenberg and Goldstein (the closest approach to a boyhood idyll in *Boyhood*) reveal both a lifelong contrarian impulse and an instinctive affinity with bullied outsiders. After playing cricket and wrestling with Goldstein and Greenberg, the narrator reflects: "I have never been happier in my life. I would like to be with Greenberg and Goldstein forever" (25).

Queer potentiality resurfaces in in the narrator's recall of a high school friend, the Greek boy Theo Stavropoulos. "He likes the look of Theo, likes his fine skin and his high coloring and his impeccable haircuts and the suave way he wears his clothes. Even the school blazer, with its silly vertical stripes, looks good on him" (148). Theo's father owns a factory. He could afford to send Theo to any school in Cape Town, but Theo, because he is "foreign," has to attend St. Joseph's, "a kind of basket to catch boys who fit nowhere else" (148). The Stavropoulos boys "are brought to school in the mornings in the blue Buick, driven sometimes by their mother but more often by a chauffeur in a peaked cap" (148). The Buick is "reputed to be the only car in Cape Town—perhaps in South Africa—with automatic gears" (148). Theo begins to teach the protagonist Ancient Greek in class until the teacher interrupts to forbid it, possibly because he is aware of the implications of "learning Greek." Because of his elegant suavity, Theo is (naturally) reputed to be a *moffie*.

This whole itinerary of difference from John is also one of enviable precocity and coolness. The term "cool" does not appear, as far as I know, in Coetzee's lexicon, and I would not expect to find it there. Yet the protagonist of *Boyhood* is drawn, even erotically drawn, to this self-possessed, stylish, cosmopolitan figure, effortlessly rising above the petty constraints of provincial education. Learning Ancient Greek seems like a route to another life.

The alter-ego figure of Theo in *Boyhood* does appear to represent an option both entertained and foreclosed. The foreclosure is partly economic, but perhaps also psychic: the narrator never puts to the test the proposition that Theo is a *moffie*, despite the fact made explicit in *Boyhood* that the narrator's first erotic objects are boys. What thus remains foreclosed is entry not just into same-sex relations but also into a world of stylish camp and queer sensibility, both with serious artistic potential. For Coetzee, that remained the road not taken. Given the range of significations now attaching to "queer," however, noting this parting of the ways is hardly tantamount to closing down all avenues of queer affect, reading, or interpretation in Coetzee's fiction.[9]

One thing "boyhood" meant in South Africa was not just finding ones level in the imperial hierarchy but also finding or being assigned ones identity, often through a process of sorting out. The first cut, mentioned in *Boyhood* was that between English and Afrikaans speaking children. That separation was a development of apartheid, under which even distinctions between whites began to be legislated at the school level. One of Coetzee's most acute anxieties was that of being classified as Afrikaans on account of his name and thus assigned to the "purgatory" of an Afrikaans medium school. One reason why I attended a convent boarding school in my early childhood was that the state schools in the region *were* Afrikaans medium, with a reputation for brutality and therefore unthinkable.

The next separation Coetzee mentions was the one between "Jews Catholics and Christians." That cut leads him to elect Catholicism and consort with Jews, one advantage of which was exemption from Protestant religious instruction. I momentarily experienced this benefit myself in one of the convents I attended. Without knowing why, I was told to go outside (with two boys named Raphael and Leon) during the Catholic mass. The nuns had identified me as Jewish. My parents soon corrected this error, which, however proved not to be an error in due course.

I was unaware that the narrative of descent circulating in my family when I was a child was marked by at least one significant omission. The British family heritage to which we laid claim included English, Irish, Scottish, and Welsh, with a small admixture of French. The Jewish history on my mother's side of the family was simply never mentioned, although my grandmother, mother, and I certainly "looked Jewish" enough, on which basis the nuns had presumably made their assignment. I am unsure why this history was suppressed during my childhood, but assume that it had to do with the assimilationist pressures of the political culture, with escaping stigma, with a desire to fit in. It also had to do with the fact that my maternal grandmother was orphaned at the age of sixteen and summarily uprooted to the home of her elder sister and brother in law in Durban, he being a militant nonconformist, with zero tolerance for Jewishness. Curious residues of my grandmother's childhood remained: one was her impassioned declamation of Shylock's speech "Hath not a Jew eyes?" and another was the occasional use of terms (*shlmazl, momzer*) that I later learned were Yiddish. She was literate without a formal education. That literacy had been acquired when, as a child of parents who had emigrated from Poland during the 1890s, she had grown up reading books in the middle of nowhere, specifically in what was not yet even Rhodesia. The cigarettes sold to black customers who were not literate in English came in large crates accompanied by coupons that could be redeemed for English classics. The children thus read the standard fiction of the time—Dickens, Thackeray—that arrived after a long sea-voyage from England. This now strikes me as a "Jewish" story, another hidden history of "white" South Africa.

When, at the convent, my parents informed the nuns they were wrong I was, although still not Catholic, obliged to attend Catholic mass. Having been reclassified as Anglican (he purely nominal religion of my parents) I was additionally required to attend Anglican Sunday school. One disapproving nun informed me that not God but Henry VIII had founded the "English" Church. I was nevertheless shipped off to this heathen institution, which at that time brought an aura of Anthony Trollope into the South African mix (mild, visibly impoverished, genteel clergy from the "old country," with real English accents). The Anglican plot thickened as I later became aware of the English missionaries from Jane Furse Hospital in Sekukhuniland, who visited my family on our farm at Steelpoort,[10] as did the Dutch Dr. Jacobs, a periodic visitor, attired in the nattiest suit and spats despite the tropical heat.

Not even in the field of "white" identities and differences can the protagonist of *Boyhood* be wholly oblivious of black or Colored people, the latter especially since he knows that their Khoisan ancestors are historic denizens of the Western Cape, predating the whites. Indeed, in his perception, the Colored people of the Boland are not even of mixed race:

> He is expert enough in physiognomy, has been expert as long as he can remember, to know that there is not a drop of white blood in them. They are Hottentots pure and uncorrupted. Not only do they come with the land, the land comes with them, is theirs, has always been (62).

Blacks, in contrast, are "latecomers." Brought to the Cape to do heavy labor under a blazing sun, "they are men without women, without children, who arrive from nowhere and can be made to disappear into nowhere" (62). They are nevertheless like the third brother in a parable, informed by the story of the Good Samaritan, on which the youthful protagonist keeps reflecting:

> It is the third brother, the humblest and most derided, who, after the first and second brothers have disdainfully passed by, helps the old woman to carry her heavy load or draws the thorn from the lion's paw. The third brother is kind and honest and courageous, while the first and second brothers are boastful, arrogant, uncharitable. At the end of the story the third brother is crowned prince, while the first and second brothers are disgraced and sent packing . . . the parallel is inescapable: the Natives [i.e., specifically the blacks in white South African parlance] are the third brother (65).

These reflections are unquestionably idiosyncratic rather than generic, and precocious for someone of that age living in that time and place. The protagonist's ironized expertise in physiognomy enables him to attribute uncorrupted purity to the "Hottentots." The parable's simple inversion of racial hierarchy may be taken as the boy's first, benevolent, step towards rejecting the dominant ideology of white racial purity and supremacy, but it hardly represents an escape from racial thinking. Perhaps there is no subjective escape, ever, in so heavily racialized a society as that of South Africa. It seems to me that both *Boyhood* and Coetzee's work at least up to *Disgrace* try to "work through" race by means that include refusing to apply reified racial labels to fictional characters in a South African context in which such labeling is the primary mode of identification and recognition. Whatever there is to be said about Coetzee's racialized consciousness (for access to which we have to rely to a large degree on his quasi-confessional writing) and his racialized representation or non-representation, he steadfastly refuses the easy option of being merely *bien pensant.*

Almost needless to say, the Coetzee of *Boyhood* has powerfully formative yet difficult relationships with both his parents, especially his mother, Vera. In one important respect, the family situation was a generic one of the time, and not only in South Africa. In the absence of men-folk fighting "up north" in World War II, women often became the anchors of the family, but, as the family disciplinarians, were also readily cast as domineering harpies. Children often encountered their fathers for the first time, as I did, only when they were several years old, having enjoyed the exclusive attention of their mothers. Returning fathers were therefore not necessarily welcome. The protagonist in *Boyhood* says: "Even before he knew his father, that is to say, before his father returned from the war, he had decided he was not going to like him" (43). Deciding that consciously hardly does justice to the oedipal fury unleashed by returning fathers. Moreover, veterans frequently returned to social failure and disappointment; wives bore the burden, as they had done during the war on the pittance paid to servicemen. (The Coetzees experienced real poverty.) A contradiction thus emerged in the specific post-World War II juncture between the supposedly immemorial patriarchal norm of family life and the social fact: "His father, if his father were to take control, would turn them into a normal family" (8). That will never happen. Instead, the protagonist guiltily engages with his father in standard routines of male bonding and female abjection that merely betray their weakness. The father-and-son narratives of *Boyhood* and *Summertime* are ineluctably ones of compromised white South African "manhood."

> December after December he and his father come to the farm to hunt. They catch . . . the ordinary passenger train, the one that stops at all the stations, even the most obscure, and sometimes has to creep into sidings and wait until

the more famous expresses have flashed past. He loves this slow train, loves sleeping snug and tight under the crisp white sheets and navy blue blankets that the bedding attendant brings, loves waking in the middle of the night at some quiet station in the middle of nowhere, hearing the hiss of the engine at rest, and the clang of the ganger's hammer as he tests the wheels (88).

The details are certainly "accurate," as I recall, but the glow of pleasure in this description has to do with the fact that the train is heading for the farm, that hunting (or pretend-hunting) allows him to share manliness with his father, and that the very slowness of the train allows the coming visit to be savored in anticipation. The train journey itself belongs to idyllic memory of a time when mobility was restricted and train journeys an occasion; when luxuries like the crisp white sheets and navy blue blankets of the South African Railways sleepers were a marked departure from ordinary life. Despite the long delays they connoted, the hissing steam engine and clink of the ganger's hammer were established pleasures of the journey.[11]

These pleasures were familiar to me from overnight trips to and from boarding school, especially savored on the return home. Even "manly" bonding with adult fellow passengers made the trip feel like a grown up experience, notably on one occasion when the two men with whom I was sharing a compartment bit off beer-bottle caps with their teeth. Such as it was, the boy farm idyll as I experienced it differed in many respects from the one evoked in Coetzee's writings. Perhaps that idyll belongs more to the Cape, to the mythicized Karroo, and to Afrikaner culture than it does to English culture, with its legacy of popular big game, action, and adventure narratives.[12]

The farm on which I grew up was situated in the far north east of the country, in the province then known as the Transvaal, now Mpumalanga. Different from the aridly beautiful Karroo, this countryside was a rugged one of indigenous thorn-bushes, rocks, scrub, and African hardwoods. it was also extremely fertile, and anything could be grown on it under irrigation: citrus, tobacco, cotton, alfalfa, wheat, vegetables. Drought was, in fact, the nemesis of single-family farming, since rainfall was marginal and irrigation expensive; in the end, it required the resources of government or agribusiness to make farming consistently profitable. During my teens, my parents simply gave up and moved elsewhere. In any event, my tranquilly recalled farm childhood had a sequel that tells a real story about South Africa.

For me, the remembered qualities of the farm are indeed ones of feudal wellbeing, with harmonious relations between blacks and whites. Guests were free to drop in at any time, and stay for months if they chose. Unlimited hospitality was expected and given. I played with black children and learned their language, mostly Sesotho, which I have now forgotten. The effect of stable tranquility was only heightened by periodic social calls from the solitary mounted policeman whose beat covered hundreds of square miles. No threat was apparent.

Yet although I could never have thought of black people as aliens in that part of the country, I had little inkling of their lives, history, and culture, or even, in fact, of their real economic position as farm workers. I was therefore totally unprepared for the fact that the Sekukhuniland region in which the farm was situated became one of the worst killing fields in the ANC-IFP (Inkhata Freedom Party, led by Gatsha Buthelezi) wars of the 1990s. Clearly, the white-boy's idyll of the farm belied unfathomed social and political realities. That was true even in the area around Creighton in Kwazulu-Natal where my parents later farmed. Political unrest had been continuously on the rise; one could even feel a trace of sympathy on occasion for the three or four South African policemen trying to keep apart a large number of black demonstrators and a pub-inflamed group of armed, white farmers. Again, I was blind-sided, however, when that area too became an ANC-IFP killing field in the early 1990s. Later, "farm-killing"—i.e., the killing of white farmers—to which Coetzee alludes in *Disgrace* became a fact of post-apartheid life.[13] As regards the latter, Jonny Steinberg's *Midlands* gives the best account I know of white obliviousness of the histories and motivations of the black people by whom they are surrounded. What seems like a farm-killing right out of the blue proves to be rooted in a long, complex history in which black people have specific land-ownership claims dating back at least to the nineteenth century. For whites, all that has been inconsequential and therefore unrecognized.

The undoing of *Boyhood's* hunting idyll entails nothing as dramatic as the eruption of virtual civil war. Father-son bonding through hunting is already a charade in the book, and of course Coetzee Sr. does not own the farm. His failure as a lawyer is compounded by the barroom bonhomie others are quick to exploit. The appearances he tries to keep up are betrayed in ways of which he has no inkling. The narrator in *Boyhood* merely remarks that his father pronounced "thirty" as "thutty." Although common (or *because* common) that pronunciation mostly signified the native speaker of Afrikaans, not English. "Thutty" sets the teeth of the youthful protagonist on edge: not only can his father not really pass for English but apparently never be a respectable parent. In contrast, despite her Afrikaner heritage and general clumsiness, his mother's spoken and written English are mysteriously flawless, no doubt a decisive fact in the history of the son who became a writer. The father's dabbling in English high culture (*Macbeth*, Wordsworth) elicits no sympathy from the son, but only embarrassment.

Partly connected to the failure of the father in *Boyhood* are the social details the autobiography conveys in a mortified, laconic voice, and in a manner reminiscent of class-conscious English fiction. The book begins "on a housing estate outside Worcester" (1) (the phrase is practically a story in itself), a town situated seventy-five miles from Cape Town. We learn later that the family has moved there from suburban Cape Town in what is clearly a class-drop brought about by the professional failure of Coetzee senior. This residential tract, inferior even to the older middle class areas of Worcester, carries the markers of white South African racial privilege without the substance: the outbuilding known as "the servant's room" houses no servant, but functions as a storeroom for trash. The "servant" in this household will be John's mother.

Later, the family returns to Cape Town, where John and his mother learn their class position. They are not "real" English residing in the fancy suburbs but in déclassé Plumstead. As distinct from the real English, they are impecunious, Anglicized Cape Anglo-Afrikaners, neither one thing nor another. Their social position, which interviewing headmasters obliquely seek to determine, means that, despite his superior academic record, John will not be admitted to the private schools attended by the real English. He must settle for the Catholic school St. Joseph's, such schools being on a distinctly lower rung than the Anglican private schools or even their state-school counterparts attended by the real English. The colonial British class system thus supervenes upon black-white hierarchy, segregation, and domination, and, in a sense, with more material consequences for white youth.

The straitened circumstances of the Coetzee family dictate that they should install a poultry run in their Worcester back yard; they need the eggs. (The real English in Cape Town would buy their eggs, and would never dream of polluting their residential space with a poultry run.) Yet the hens do not lay in this setting, and indeed develop "gross swellings." Coetzee's aunt tells his mother that the hens will not lay until "the horny shells under their tongues have been cut out" (1). This intrusion of obscene grotesquerie belongs to the abject lifestyle, taking on almost Gothic proportions:

> So one after another his mother takes the hens between her knees, presses on their jowls till they open their beaks, and with the point of a paring-knife picks at their tongues. The hens shriek and struggle, their eyes bulging. He shudders and turns away. He thinks of his mother slapping stewing-steak down on the kitchen counter and cutting it into cubes; he thinks of her bloody fingers (1–2).

If this episode is the traumatic primal scene of Coetzee's later vegetarianism, its horror is, as always, partly a matter of perspective; Vera and her sister are closer than the shuddering boy to South Africa's agrarian past and to farm people's phlegmatically cruel treatment of animals. Yet the suburban mother with blood on her hands will forever remain imprinted on her son's mind. She is not even his real mother, but his "second mother," the first one being the passionately loved Karroo farm Voëlfontein. The bad mother usurps upon the powers of the oedipal father and wields a knife that carries with it distant threats of muting and castration. The son who "shudders and turns away" is already enacting the aversion and dissociation that will become lifelong traits. Coetzee senior later—"jokingly"—compares Vera and her sisters to the witches in *Macbeth*. Neither son can bring himself to address Vera as "mother"; they somehow hit on the sisterly nickname Dinny.

In later life, Coetzee seemed captive to what *Boyhood* evokes here as a backyard Gothic melodrama featuring his mother above all. I have already remarked that it was not easy to correlate the unassertive, worn, elderly grandmother I met with the looming Clytemnestra of Coetzee's anecdotes. Yet in addition to being the bloody butcher in the kitchen, the Dinny of *Boyhood* appears in many guises, and the son's relation to her is tonally and affectively complex. These guises include the sacrificial mother devoted to, and guiltily spurned by, her favored older son; the perplexing authority-figure the son struggles to understand; the housebound, abjected woman and spouse whose purchase of a bicycle to expand her range elicits both sympathy and chagrin; the strong wife regarded with disfavor by her weak husband's extended family; the formative parent with whom the boy Coetzee enjoys an intense special relationship that makes his brother David a rival. Being "chosen" by the mother becomes a self-fulfilling prophecy of later success.

The final form of boyhood induction I wish to consider in *Boyhood* is the induction of postwar white South African youth into the "adult" politics of the country. Those politics included the Cold War and the rise of Afrikaner nationalism. It had become risky for anyone to avow Russian sympathies, yet the already disaffected young Coetzee secretly sides with the Russians against the Americans.

In the public world, Afrikaner nationalism after 1948 increasingly traded on the Communist "threat" to justify any repressive legislation or suppression of black resistance (an effective strategy for garnering support from the United States and the European powers). Although a mere five seats obtained the Nationalist victory in 1948, its permanence was guaranteed in short order, as noted in *Boyhood*, by gerrymandering that increased the proportional power of rural, Afrikaner constituencies in general elections. This party remained in power through the ending of apartheid in 1994.

The difference this victory made to black and Colored people mattered, since under N.P. rule apartheid laws were ruthlessly systematized, enforced and expanded. Following some local electoral losses in the Cape, for which Colored voters were held responsible, a newly "packed" Senate voted to separate them from white voters and remove them from the common voting roll in 1956. They would henceforth be represented by a small number of elected whites, although in the late stages of apartheid they had their "own" legislature, as did blacks in the so-called Bantustans. Population transfers mandated under the Group Areas Act of 1957 occurred ever more frequently, on a larger scale. The hapless United Party, led at that point by J.G.N. Strauss (whose hand, I now recall with amusement, I once shook as a child) squirmed and protested within the limits of its own segregationist policy, yet it offered nothing more to black, Colored, and Indian voters than apartheid lite, of which they had already had more than enough.[14] The protagonist's father in *Boyhood* is the United Party "type," but sees the writing on the wall: "Advocate Strauss, the new leader of the United Party, is only a pale shadow of Smuts; under Strauss, the UP has no hope of winning the next election" (68).

White political consciousness, then, remained largely limited to the parliamentary struggle between "Nats." and "U.P." The U.P. represented both English and Afrikaans voters, and many of its members, like the *Boyhood* narrator's father, had served in World War II. The Nats in contrast, were a militantly exclusive Afrikaner party, a number of whose leading members had been interned during World War II for their avowed Nazi sympathies (in a cruel irony, German Jews on the political left were sometimes interned along with them as enemy aliens). Many Nats were also members of the secret Afrikaner Broederbond (Brotherhood) widely believed to be the real power in national politics.

In one aspect, these Nat-U.P. politics were a charade distracting attention from the real struggle of black and white, the latter struggle kept out of white view as much as possible. In another aspect, however, they were fuelled by significant antipathies. Antifascist ex-servicemen, a number of whom later made their way into the African National Congress as associates of Nelson Mandela, formed the nucleus of a nonracial left opposition to the Nationalist Government. The more conservative Torch Commando, formed in 1951 to resist the removal of Colored voters from the common roll, attracted a significant following among ex-servicemen and well-placed professionals. This was potentially serious politics, yet ingrained hostility to Afrikaners sufficed for most English speaking U.P. members. Mockery was the weapon of choice. Scandalous stories circulated of the antics of naked, drunken parliamentarians.

Conflating "Afrikaner" with "Nat" was virtually a reflex of English-speaking South Africans in the period after 1948, yet this was not a conflation possible for Coetzee, with his sense of a divided, bilingual heritage, whatever aversion he may have felt towards Afrikaner bullies. Pointedly, he wrote the dialogues between Magda and Hendrik in the first South African edition (Ravan) of *In the Heart of the Country* in Afrikaans. The dialogues are written with an idiomatic mastery and sureness of touch foreign to the vast majority of "English" South Africans. Coetzee's bilingualism then enabled him to translate these dialogues into English for the international Penguin edition. As Magda notes, these dialogues proceed in the seemingly immemorial, codified Afrikaans exchanged between masters and servants on farms. Magda also observes that this language has been corrupted by her father's improprieties with Hendrik's wife. In the context in which the novel was written, however, any heralded failure of these Afrikaans codes of exchange is momentous: they herald the ending of an "old order." That is an order still largely presumed in the political education—or miseducation—of white youth in *Boyhood*, but the presumption is already obsolete.

To conclude, then, I began this chapter by emphasizing the generic dimensions of *Boyhood*. It is also obviously, however, the fictionalized autobiography of a highly singular individual. Readers will inevitably scour the book for clues about the origins of Coetzee's creativity and distinctive authorial "profile." *De facto, Boyhood* and *Youth* are portraits of the artist as a young man (although Coetzee would balk at the designation "artist"), and must consciously be so, in a tradition descending not only from James Joyce but Leo Tolstoy. Notably, Coetzee does not make this the autobiography of a *Wunderkind*, marked out from the beginning for fame and fortune, although scattered indications of precocity, intense rivalry, or preternatural awareness make the boy "special," as does his mother's favor. *Boyhood* allows us to see Coetzee's work as the complex outcome of negative stimuli more than positive ones, namely experiences of pain, mortification, confinement, familial dysfunction, the life of the provinces, pervasive negative affect. Such are among the promptings to take flight in both senses of the term, and they are not necessarily the promptings associated with the idealized "artist."

Boyhood's pain and "negativity" have led many readers to regard the book as grim, as I did initially. On the one occasion on which I heard Coetzee read it in public, however, at Dartmouth College, his inflections brought out the mordant humor of *Boyhood* and, implicitly, the comic persona inhabiting it. One might suggest that humor and irony are underrated features of Coetzee's writing in general, belied by the generally solemn and often awestruck tenor of its academic reception, but the humor of *Boyhood* allows Coetzee at once to revive and keep his distance from the painful circumstances so sharply imprinted on our minds by the book.

NOTES

1. Rudyard Kipling, "Recessional," *Complete Verse* (New York: Anchor Books, 1989), 327.
2. On this topic, as well as that of Coetzee's represented beginnings as a writer, see Lars Engle, "Being Literary in the Wrong Way, Time and Place," *English Studies in Africa*, 49, 2: 47.
3. J.M Coetzee, *Age of Iron* (New York: Random House, 1990), 28–29. In characterizing this Afrikaner ruling class as one engaged in "slow peasant plots that take decades to mature," Coetzee interestingly emphasizes primitive rural antecedents, yet at the expense of the distinctly twentieth century participation of that ruling class in in the sphere of advanced international capitalism, including its corruption and scandals. The rise of Afrikaner nationalism after 1948 was as much an economic as a political phenomenon.

4. *The Land of Lost Content: The Biography of Anthony Chenevix-Trench (London: Pentland* (London: Pentland, 1996)

5. Perhaps Coetzee's experience and representation of shame (and of "negative affect" more generally) can be understood to some degree in the framework supplied by Timothy Bewes, *The Event of Postcolonial Shame* (Princeton: Princeton University Press, 2010).

6. Namely, the Royal Irish Constabulary Reserve Force recruited to fight the IRA during the Irish War of Independence. The force included many World War 1 veterans, and was notorious for its brutality to civilians.

7. Wulf Sachs, *Black Hamlet* (1937) (New York: Kessinger Reprints, 2010).

8. After his release, Finkelstein, a paraplegic in a wheelchair, went on to become a prominent activist in England on behalf of the handicapped.

9. But see Elleke Boehmer, "Coetzee's Queer Body," *Journal of Literary Studies*, 21, 3–4 (2005), 222–34. In *Boyhood*, boys first stir Coetzee's preadolescent desire, to which experience he learns to apply the term "perversion" (61).

10. Actually, two adjacent farms, Watanope and Eerstegeluk, originally owned by the prominent Johannesburg architect, J.A. Moffat, who turned increasingly to farming in semi-retirement. My grandmother, Jean Morgan, had been his longtime secretary, and effectively became his nurse-housekeeper as his health declined. On his death, he left her the farms. I recall his small memorial on a stone hillock near the farmhouse, with this inscription from *Macbeth* on the tombstone: "After life's fitful fever/ He sleeps well."

11. Intense, lyrical recall of the childhood train journey may have been constituted as a literary trope by Vladimir Nabokov, "First Love," *The Portable Nabokov*, ed. Page Stegner (New York: Viking Press, 1971), 179–89. There, the upscale wagon-lit train runs from St. Petersburg to Paris, the provinces to the capital.

12. For an interesting and well-illustrated overview of this hunting and exploration culture, see Bartle Bull, *Safari: A Chronicle of Adventure* (New York: Viking, 1988).

13. Jonny Steinberg, *Midlands* (Cape Town: Jonathan Ball, 2002),

14. Smuts himself, an erstwhile Boer War General, world statesman, World War II associate of Winston Churchill, and a founding figure in the United Nations, began to develop second thoughts when it became clear that South Africa's racial policies would not meet the standard of nonracial democracy espoused by the United Nations.

Chapter Five

Disgrace

Coetzee's autobiographical trilogy narrates the transition from boyhood to youth, that transition being marked by, among other things, sexual initiation, emigration along the beaten colonial track to London, professional employment in the computer industry, and serious dedication to the project of becoming a writer. Already as a schoolboy, and then as a student at UCT, Coetzee had manifested literary aspirations. Kannemeyer (630-32) cites in full a long, vastly ambitious creation-poem titled "In The Beginning," written by Coetzee as a sixteen-year-old schoolboy. Both the ambition and the level of accomplishment are remarkable. Kannemeyer also reproduces (100-02) some poems Coetzee published as a student at the university of Cape Town, further noting that Coetzee was the dominant figure in a group of talented student poets, including Daniel Hutchinson and Jonty Driver, in Cape Town.

Like the title "Boyhood," "Youth" plays against codified expectations. The "youth" represented here is largely characterized by alienation, depression and isolation in the metropolis, not by high spirits, *joie de vivre*, or promise of high accomplishment. It is in London that Coetzee discovers that others in the computer business are his superiors in mathematics, and that he will never be a creative mathematician.

The malaise of Coetzee's youth was certainly one possible outcome of the relocation of young South Africans to a London that had previously existed for them only in fiction and myth. Other young people from the "Commonwealth" were adrift in the same predicament. The Coetzee of *Youth* befriends Ganapathy, an Indian worker in the same computer business as Coetzee, who tries to subsist on a diet of bananas. The hapless Ganapathy mirrors the narrator's own abysmal condition. If there is a way out, it lies in the direction of the United States and of the academic career, a trajectory that was abruptly reversed, however, by Coetzee's deportation from the United States in 1971, back to the middle of nowhere.

Published in 1999, *Disgrace* makes a major impact almost at once; I soon notice it on sale in airports, a sign of mass-market success. On reading the book, I am on the lookout for clues about how Coetzee is negotiating the world of post-boyhood and post-apartheid South Africa. My contacts with him since 1974 have almost all been abroad, leaving me with little sense of how he is faring at home. In *The Life and Times of Michael K.*, the solitary, fugitive protagonist muses: "I am becoming smaller, harder, drier every day" (93). To me, Coetzee's persona has seemed increasingly fugitive, ascetic, and severe as time has passed, although not on that account unfriendly or forbidding.

The narrative of David Lurie in *Disgrace* is not strictly autobiographical, yet as an aging male academic who teaches Romanticism,[1] Lurie obviously exists in suggestive proximity to Coetzee. Again the "voices" of character and author merge. The narrative also registers personal concerns that have evidently developed for Coetzee over time: the difficulty of being a father; preoccupation with aging and mortality; a sense of being professionally out of place and redundant in the "Cape Technical University," at once a thinly veiled representation of the University of Cape Town and a projection of its future in a world in which the traditional humanities have been superseded. "English" has largely been reduced to Communications teaching. When Lurie retires, his Romantics course will presumably disappear. He and his few remaining elderly colleagues in literature have become redundant "clerks in a post-religious age" (4).

The book also suggests that, for Coetzee, South Africa is becoming harder to read and write:

> More and more he is convinced that English is an unfit medium for the truth of South Africa. Stretches of English code whole sentences long have thickened, lost their articulations, their articulateness, their articulatedness. Like a dinosaur expiring and settling in the mud, the language has stiffened. Pressed into the mould of English, Petrus's story would come out arthritic, bygone" (117).

These reflections, infused with Coetzee's hypersensitivity to language, have the thought-provoking force of a general statement, yet they are also distinctly a function of Lurie's predicament. The career of the novelist Zakes Mda (an admirer, let it be said, of Coetzee's writing) suggests that there are other ways of writing South Africa, and other versions of English, not necessarily subject to this expiration. Mda's breeziness and humor suggest the advantages of lightening up, while also suggesting that comedy offers surprising resources for "post-traumatic" writing (the trauma of Xhosa history; the trauma of the AIDS epidemic).[2] It may not necessarily be English as such but the unrelentingly fastidious, high-cultural codes of Coetzee's writing that have become problematic in South Africa (or always were so).

Lurie's narrative records the premature onset of aging, at least at the level of his consciousness. He is only fifty-two, yet feels superannuated, and his young male rival for Melanie's affections taunts him with his age. He, along with everyone else, is aware of the inappropriateness of his relationship with a woman young enough to be his daughter or even granddaughter. His former wife is especially scathing. Concerns with aging, mortality (including "ways of dying," as Zakes Mda might put it), and, sometimes, relations to younger women, recur in Coetzee's post-*Disgrace* fiction. Coetzee even crosses the threshold into "posthumous" writing in *Summertime.* That he can do so is no great paradox: insofar as Coetzee's life is a life "in" writing, he can pursue his own self-inscription beyond the grave. While *Disgrace* does not "explain" Coetzee's emigration to Australia, it does convey a profound sense of displacement that makes emigration intelligible.

Having never lived in post-apartheid South Africa, I track its fortunes from a distance through the media, but also during visits and through information from my mother and two brothers, she having been an anti-Apartheid activist and a Robben Island prison visitor in the Black Sash women's organization, while my bother Adrian had been employed in the ANC ministry of transport. My brother Robin worked as an academic dean at the University of Pretoria during the critical transition from apartheid. They are all sufficiently connected to be reliable informants. I am also curious, however, to see that political world refracted through the consciousness of Coetzee's Lurie.

I soon learn that *Disgrace* has stirred controversy in and out of South Africa. I read that members of the ANC government have complained to the 1999 Human Rights Commission on Racism in the Media that the representation of three black men as rapists in *Disgrace* perpetuates negative stereotyping and revives the inflammatory "black peril" rhetoric of former white nationalism. (Can this fact disturbingly help to explain the book's mass-market appeal?) The term "Lucy syndrome" shortly emerges to characterize the character Lucy's seeming acquiescence in rape to atone for the historic crimes of her people. Writing in 2000, Athol Fugard remarks that the notion of white women's submitting to rape as a form of atonement is "a load of bloody bullshit."[3]

In fact, the representation of the male rapists and Lucy's seeming acquiescence seem disconcerting and inevitably provocative to me on first reading of the novel. I must assume, however, that Coetzee has made a deliberate choice, since he could hardly be more aware of the troping of the "colored" rapist in Anglo-colonial fiction starting with Shakespeare's *The Tempest* and continuing through E. M. Forster's *A Passage to India* and Paul Scott's *Raj Quartet*. Nor can he unaware of how black peril rhetoric has been exploited throughout South African political history, not to mention in the American south. *Disgrace* can never be fully extricated from that history. Its representation of Lucy's rape cannot therefore be presented as an innocently realist account of the post-apartheid rape epidemic in South Africa. In any event, any suggestion of innocent realism in his writing makes Coetzee's hackles rise. I once remarked to him that I was unaware that he knew the Eastern Cape region in which the novel concludes. He retorted that he did not know it: it was all made up. At this, Dorothy Driver, who was also present, reacted incredulously. On a recent trip to South Africa (2015), my brother pointed out an animal shelter near Salem in the Eastern Cape, supposed by locals to be the original for the animal shelter in *Disgrace*. Nevertheless, Coetzee's strenuous disavowals of realism, not to mention his metafictional practice, preclude any defense of *Disgrace* on the basis of transparent realism.

In social fact, post-apartheid rape, mostly perpetrated by black men on women and children of color, includes so-called corrective rape directed at lesbians, to "teach them what women are."[4] The protagonist, David Lurie, speculates about this possible motive for the rape of his daughter. Commentary on *Disgrace* additionally notes that David Lurie's "not quite" (25) rape of the student Melanie, who is marked although not named as colored in *Disgrace*, reiterates a long history of sexual violence perpetrated on women of color by colonial white men. Those are presumably the "overtones" to which one member of the committee inquiring into Lurie's conduct refers, and of which Lurie denies the existence. The rape of the protagonist's daughter thus supposedly turns the tables, yet the politics of tit-for-tat are far from delivering the justice sought in South Africa, both through and beyond the Truth and Reconciliation Commission.[5]

The amount of world-attention once focused on apartheid-era South Africa makes it understandable that many readers, myself included, would want a report on the post-apartheid situation beyond the initial moment of rainbow-nation euphoria. The term "dysfunctional postcolony" has increasingly been used to characterize the "new" South Africa both in fact and as represented in *Disgrace*. That is clearly a post-apartheid development in both critical and political discourse. When, for example, Coetzee published *Age of Iron* in 1990, the familiar lineaments of apartheid were still in evidence, although the government had been under increasing pressure since 1976, when the Soweto riots produced an increasingly ungovernable population, especially of militant black youth. The South Africa of *Disgrace* is indeed "new," a fact confirmed for me when I visited both after the publication of the book and recently (2015). The advent of walled-in, gated, middle class homes, all bearing signs that they are protected by rapid-response armed security services, implied the collapse of public law and order. I was amused to note one of these signs posted on the windowless citadel of the Fish Hoek police station on the Cape Peninsula. Evidently the police could no longer protect themselves, let alone others, a point made in *Disgrace*.

Some of the promise of the new South Africa had also clearly been realized: the signs of legal segregation had all disappeared, and formerly segregated spaces, like public beaches, were now integrated. On Fish Hoek beach, my brother and I watched a Muslim Imam in long robes playing with his children in the surf. My brother remarked on how strange it was that a mere few years ago people killed to prevent this.[6] Students of color are now visibly the majority in public schools and universities, including the University of Cape Town. Signs of the new order are evident in *Disgrace*, where the senior university personnel are now multi-ethnic, as are the students. Affluence is more widely distributed among different ethnic communities, including the so-called Black Diamonds, the class of extremely affluent blacks that has emerged since the end of apartheid. Possibly in keeping with the dynamics of neoliberalism, the South Africa of today exhibits a increasingly glaring gap between affluence and poverty, with opulent gentrification occurring in many urban centers and seaside resorts. Juxtaposed black poverty is still glaringly evident in what were formerly called shanty towns, now called Informal Housing settlements, like Khayelitsha near Cape Town. All this is evident to me as a virtual tourist in what had formerly been "home." Deeper and more complex realities of the new South Africa, whatever they may be, remain unseen, although as its narrative "deepens," *Disgrace* offers some hints.

As time goes on, the controversy surrounding *Disgrace* diminishes but does not wholly die out. One American colleague, of South African origin, says she cannot bear to reread the book because its seigneurial gender-politics make her so angry. Another colleague, this one American, complains that Coetzee, being cool, has moved beyond the banalities of Political Correctness, yet only to recycle unreconstructed race and gender representations. A more favorable view comes from one book-jacket reviewer, who opines that *Disgrace* "teaches us what it is to be human." This reviewer neglects to add that if the book teaches what it is to be human, it does so by asking what it is to be human at the expense of animals. In any event, I do not consider it my brief to attack or defend *Disgrace*. The question for me, and perhaps *mutatis mutandis* for Coetzee, is how to relate my past to this present.

Disgrace begins within the familiar precincts of the University of Cape Town and within the recognizable, and somewhat disarming, conventions of the campus novel. These are essentially comic conventions that trade on college gossip, scandal, politics, and romantic entanglements. Both the protocols of disciplinary investigation and the language of bureaucratic communication in the novel conform to recognizable international norms of the academy. The codes governing sexual harassment, of which Lurie falls foul, are standard Western ones, although as applied here intruding "overtones" give the hearing a seriousness and bitterness somewhat foreign to the campus novel. Lurie not only rejects the codified solution of a leave of absence and "counseling," but the premises of the entire collegiate mechanism of repentance and restitution. He thereby forfeits his position and forestalls the conventional happy ending to the academic comedy.

Distanced from the present generation of students, Lurie regards them as "Post-Christian, posthistorical, postliterate, they might as well have been hatched from eggs yesterday" (32). Although willing to give high Romantic poetry a go, Lurie's student Melanie, like so many contemporary students, has voted with her feet by becoming engaged in performance and acting. Although not without literary susceptibility, the "clever" (168) Melanie becomes animated and reveals her talent as an actress and mimic in the low farce, *Sunset at the Globe Salon*, in which Lurie watches her perform. In this representation of the new South Africa, to which Lurie lends no credence, "A hairdresser, flamboyantly gay, attends two clients, one black, and one white... catharsis seems to be the presiding principle; all the coarse old prejudices brought into the light of day and washed away in gales of laughter" (23).

Lurie's own marginalization in the college and forced relocation in the Communications Department leads him to complain that education has been "emasculated" (his term, p. 4) at the newly technocratic CTU. The perceived threat of emasculation seems present, however, not just in what has happened in education, but in his consciousness of diminished sexual attractiveness, and during the disciplinary hearing to which he is summoned on a charge of sexual harassment. Broadly, this perceived threat of emasculation, recurring throughout the novel, appears to be a function of eroded white, colonial entitlement and male narcissism in South Africa. What it would really mean to forfeit white, middle class privilege rather than just disavow it or find it somewhat impaired emerges in the second part of the novel. I can think of no other work of fiction that imagines forfeited white entitlement as starkly as *Disgrace* does. The book is crushingly anti-hubristic and chastening, a final settling of accounts, it would seem, with everything Lurie represents in the novel. His forms of superiority collapse, and his flippancies invariably backfire, as when he mocks animal rights activists, whose pieties, as he puts it, incite in him a desire to go "raping and pillaging" (73). He will find out in the novel what that means.

The Romanticism that is not only Lurie's professional stock in trade but deeply internalized—it is no accident that his daughter is named Lucy—begins by being a barely viable course topic, but once he is dismissed, it simply has no location in the new South Africa. Insofar as Lurie attempts to give it currency by, for example, proclaiming himself a servant of Eros or by quoting to Lucy the apercus of Romanticism on the prerogatives of (male) desire, there is simply no market for it. It thus becomes wholly internalized in Lurie's attempt to compose an opera on Byron and his mistress in Italy. In the course of composition, Lurie reidentifies himself, not with Byron, but with the middle aged Teresa, living on after Byron's death and howling in solitude. In the process of composition, Lurie relinquishes "lush" Straussian orchestration in favor of music picked out on the tinny, township guitar he has bought for Lucy at an earlier time. Having momentarily entertained the hope of a success redeeming his disgrace, Lurie is left with a crippled dog and jeering children as his auditors. Everything in Lurie's life gravitates towards the nadir: the story of an "old" South African in the new South Africa. I am not sorry to be witnessing Lurie's purgatorial undoing from a safe, fictional distance.

Lurie's purgatorial ordeal in the novel includes being burned-burnt, but not, it would seem, with any redemptive prospect, although some readers have wanted to see Lurie attaining grace in the end to redress his disgrace. That would tend to make the novel a hagiography of one who sins his way to heaven. Since the book does invoke religious contexts and figures like the self-castrating Origen, it may indeed owe something to the now often underrated genre of hagiography, too often understood to be a mere whitewashing enterprise.[7] If so, however, its theology seems unyieldingly negative, and its secular implication the tragic absence, post-TRC, of any mechanisms of redemption, atonement, or restitution. We hear nothing, for example, about the response of Melanie's sister and mother to Lurie's invented ritual of abasement before them, but perhaps their silence is sufficient commentary.

The process of undoing includes Lurie's poignant final relinquishment of the crippled dog to which he has become attached in the animal shelter, and which has been the sole auditor of his romantic opera. Like the other dogs whose "dignity" Lurie wishes to defend, it will have to be euthanized, but Lurie could prolong its life by a week. Bev expresses surprise when he decides not to, and asks: "Are you giving him up?" He replies, in the last sentence of the novel: "Yes, I am giving him up." Nothing, it would seem, can be held back, and no point of anchorage found for any "crippled" narcissistic identification.[8] He must accept the unadorned prospect of his own death in accepting that of the dog. That is what relinquishment means in *Disgrace*.

When the locale shifts to the Eastern Cape in *Disgrace*, the novel records the breakdown of public services, including police services and animal shelters. Life has become "dangerous" as even the black character Petrus acknowledges (at present, the ANC administration of the Eastern Cape is reputedly the worst in the country). The narrator's prediction that the neighbor Ettinger, who goes armed, will end up with a bullet in the back belongs to the new South Africa of "farm killings." The geographical shift of locale in the novel entails a generic shift into a terminally dire, practically inverted version of the farm novel (*plaasroman*). Driven out of his academic shelter, Lurie eventually finds himself (perhaps in quite a strong sense of the phrase) in the animal shelter. The novel makes demands on the reader in leading him/her beyond the reassuring confines of the campus novel. Already, the conventions of the campus novel have been disturbed, not by an affair between a professor and a student, but by a sexual-harassment hearing with strong race/gender undertones.

It is in the farm setting that the rape of Lucy occurs. That episode seems to flirt dangerously, as the ANC response implied, with a white racist stereotype, not just of black men, but of black men who "will rape your daughter." Yet the episode also insistently poses the question of how this rape is to be *read*, both in and out of a fictional lineage. For better or worse, it is as if Coetzee felt bound to confront rather than finesse this founding trope of the white racist imaginary. The confrontation is or was bound to be self-implicating, perhaps even broadly implicating to the book's readership, yet the event of rape here becomes a set piece for reading.

The primary interpretive perspective here as throughout the novel is Lurie's. In Lurie's reading, the rape becomes a heavily overdetermined event, its possible overdetermining conditions including historical revenge, the (male) reproductive imperative, archaic precedents, calculated, land-grabbing violence, and unfathomable hatred. In other words, the rape does not "read out" predictably or monolithically in the new post-apartheid world, in which, in any case, there is no longer an intelligible political purpose to be served by troping black rape. Yet the limitations of Lurie's interpretive powers are marked from the start by Lucy's refusal to name or narrate the rape, above all as the reportable legal crime Lurie wants to make it. Lurie demands a narrative Lucy utterly withholds while resisting her father's interpretive compulsion. If there is a simple fact of rape it is one Lucy will not produce, leaving it, so to speak, to her father's imagination. But there is no simple fact—humiliating violence is directed at the father as well as the daughter, and even at the dogs Lucy is boarding. In other words, *this* rape becomes a complex construction in which the reader is forced to participate along with the novel's characters.

Moreover, the rapists do not conform to local cultural or physiognomic stereotypes of black savagery, nor is the rapists' behavior out of control, except in the case of the mentally impaired youth with the mystifyingly exotic Latin name of Pollux (not, it would seem, the Romantic Shelley's "mild Pollux, void of blame"). In a departure from the white racist prototype, Lucy decides, against practically everyone's urging, to bear the child of rape. Most readers will probably concur in Lurie's urgent pleas to Lucy to have an abortion, leave the area, in which the position of a single woman is untenable, even leave the country and start over. What sensible, modern person would think otherwise? (Even people opposed to abortion tend to make an exception for rape.) Although Lucy does argue her point with her father, both she and the novel have moved into what is uncharted territory with respect to the "old" South Africa and the apartheid novel. Coetzee allows the possibility that women would understand the entire episode differently, since if Lucy shares her experience with anyone it is with Bev and with her female doctor (Lucy snaps at her father when he assumes the doctor is male).

The territory is both social and psychic. Lucy's silence presents an insuperable barrier to "understanding," and may itself be read as a traumatic aftermath. The reticence of Petrus, first Lucy's "dog man," then co-owner of the farm, then outright owner, and finally her prospective husband in what will be, for him, a polygamous marriage, presents another barrier to "understanding." An entire history, together with a language barrier, makes it impossible that Petrus, although a reasonably competent speaker of English, can be expected to speak frankly and openly with Lurie, let alone "explain." From Lurie's standpoint, the new South Africa thus becomes a place of frustrating silences against which his sophisticated monologue becomes ever more "interior." As a specialist in Communications, his own power to communicate ranges from limited to practically non-existent. Coetzee's *Foe*, where Friday's tongue has been cut out, strongly anticipates this impasse created by silence.[9]

The new social reality also eludes Lurie's comprehension. Regarding Petrus, Lurie reflects:

> The real truth . . . is something far more—he cast around for the word—*anthropological*, something it would take months to get to the bottom of, months of patient, unhurried conversation with dozens of people, and the offices of an interpreter" (118).

Perhaps anthropological understanding is no more than a fantasy that in actuality marks the failure of Lurie's interpretive powers as a literary humanist. He cannot read the new situation in terms of his own discipline.

What *is* evident to Lurie is the set of drastic reversals that have upended the old white order. The takeover of Lucy's farm by Petrus and her consenting to be taken under his protection as a polygamous wife belong, in *Disgrace*, to an older peasant order reasserting itself in the collapse of white administration. What takes the place of public law and order is the "protection" Petrus is equipped to offer, both as upwardly mobile peasant paterfamilias and as one who knows how to work the modern financial and technological systems. The reversal in which the former black employee and "dog man" displaces the white landowner presents an obvious historical irony, especially pointed since it is happening in what, as Lurie recalls, used to be "British Kaffraria" (i.e., the British colonial territory primarily inhabited by Xhosa "kaffirs"). Lurie's first becoming Petrus's help and then becoming the ultimate "dog man" at the end of the novel compounds the irony. Reversals, described by Lurie as "the stuff of bourgeois comedy" (14), do not produce the comic catharsis they aim for in Melanie's play.

In *The Story of an African Farm* (1893), Olive Schreiner modeled the classic "African farm:"

> At the foot of the kopje lay the homestead. First, the stone-walled sheep kraals and Kaffer huts; beyond them the dwelling-house—a square, red-brick building with thatched roof."[10]

Such is the physical and social topography of the African farm, with its hierarchical progression from the animals to the "Kaffers" in huts to the white landowners in a brick dwelling. This topography of the Karroo farm remains relatively stable even in the recollected Voëlfontein in *Boyhood*, with its two resident Colored families, although there, as we have seen, the young Coetzee asks to whom the land really belongs.[11]

Disgrace seems like the novel in which the story of an African farm finally comes to an end. Lucy's "farm" is already hardly that, as Lurie notes, but little more than a plot capable of sustaining market gardening and dog boarding. Another genre that comes to an end in *Disgrace*, if it has not previously done so, is the South African apartheid novel, or, more accurately, the anti-apartheid novel. By this I mean a literature of social protest or critique, much of it written, although not always by white writers, within a tradition of English political liberalism and of English fictional realism. The books fitting into this category are quite varied and formally resourceful, but what they have in common is anger and disgust at the racial politics of South Africa and their impingement on people of color. Alan Paton and Nadine Gordimer are only two of the prominent writers of the apartheid era; very little written under apartheid could break out of its enclosure or depart from its racial identities. This fiction thus tended to seal off South Africa within its own political orbit, a tendency always resisted in Coetzee's fiction. Juxtaposing historical South Africa with Vietnam-era America in *Dusklands* already expanded the geographical and chronological frame.

In retrospect, it is possible to see Coetzee's early fiction as the beginning of the end for the apartheid novel. The best evidence of that is the difficulty with which that early fiction was assimilated in South Africa: clearly, certain expectations were not being met. One response to which I have already alluded was that this fiction was not political at all, "political" then being understood only in the familiar apartheid framework of oppression, resistance, and moral outrage. Much can be said about Coetzee's radical stylistic, generic, and philosophical departures from the apartheid novel, but one such departure, pertinent to *Disgrace*, was that of removing the labels of ethnic identity to which readers of the apartheid novel (and, indeed, all South Africans) were accustomed, to the point that they had been internalized as reality. These were generally the labels attached to the reified identities of the apartheid system: white, black, Colored, Indian. Even the best-intentioned apartheid fiction tended to remain captive to this classification. An old school, white, South African expatriate friend in England complained to me that Coetzee was dishonest for not stipulating in *Disgrace* that Melanie and her family are Colored. I replied that that was the point. It is true that any reader of my generation can still "read" race (associated with class) in *Disgrace*, but the labels now belong to no "objective" reality in the novel but remain as a mental residue of prior conditioning, ghosts of history. In the apartheid novel, Lurie's opening liaison with Soraya might well be a tragic romance of racial transgression across the color line, at risk of arrest. Insofar as ethnicities come into the picture now, they do so only in the sex market for "exotic" women.

The overt politics of post-apartheid South Africa under the successive regimes of Nelson Mandela and Thabo Mbeki are present only by distant implication in *Disgrace*, almost as if they are beside the point. Despite recurrent visits to South Africa and first-hand information from residents, I do not know a great deal more about those politics than any reasonably well-informed newspaper reader. Like everyone else, I know of the AIDS epidemic that overtook the country during the 1990s, and of Thabo Mbeki's catastrophic policy of AIDS-denial. In *Disgrace*, one of David Lurie's immediate concerns after Lucy has been raped is that she may have contracted AIDS. I am aware of the horrifying testimony, and of some of the political and philosophical fallout, of the Truth and Reconciliation Commission (TRC). I am aware that the ANC government has continuing problems with the delivery of housing and basic services to the population, and I am aware that charges of widespread corruption have been leveled at the ANC, many of whose members have seized the opportunity to get rich. All these tendencies, as well as public dissatisfaction with them, have become only more pronounced under the current regime of Jacob Zuma, himself accused of large-scale corruption and misappropriation. I am aware that widespread crime has become—or has been made—a political issue. Finally, I am aware that disenchantment has succeeded euphoria in post-apartheid South Africa. Yet none of this is exactly the point in *Disgrace*.

If there is a new politics on the horizon here, it seemingly cannot materialize in the South Africa of *Disgrace*. "On the list of the nation's priorities, animals come nowhere," says Lucy (73). Yet Coetzee evidently makes the treatment of animals one index of the limits of post-apartheid liberation; it is also an index of the limits of the meaning of "political" in South Africa, old or new. The two sheep Petrus unnecessarily tethers produce an unexpected, pivotal movement of sympathy in Lurie, from which there is no going back to the brittle complacency of his initial exchange with Lucy about animal rights. Lurie's impulse to liberate the sheep (there is no question of saving them from being killed for Petrus's feast) begins to change Lurie, who has previously insisted that he is beyond counseling, beyond change, beyond reclamation. He assists Bev in the animal shelter, and also "descends" to have sex with her at her instigation, although he has previously commented on her extreme unattractiveness in his eyes. Lurie's loss of privilege evidently becomes converted into a choice and even a vocation: saving the dignity of dead dogs, through the most abject of outcast services, is hardly a politics, yet it apparently becomes, not only Lurie's way of salvaging the dignity his own disgrace has cost him, but of upholding an "idea of the world," as he puts it, characterized by decency and respect.

If, from a skeptical point of view, Lurie's quest seems increasingly solitary, personal, and even deranged in the South African context of *Disgrace*, in which "animal rights" is practically a meaningless term, it is in and through that solitary quest that a critique of South Africa's post-apartheid politics, but not only those, begins to emerge in all seriousness.[12] Coetzee discovers a new sense of mission as a person and a writer, and finds new kindred spirits, many in the international academic community. An assertion of dignity in the context of euthanasia and mechanized incineration is more than personal, since it unquestionably imports a Holocaust subtext others have noted in *Disgrace*. In the wake of *Disgrace*, Coetzee's *The Lives of Animals* appeared in 2001. In that book, Elizabeth Costello makes an explicit, contentious, connection between animal genocide and the Holocaust. Questions regarding animals and animal rights are no longer to be dismissed with Lurie's initial flippancy. They are not just questions about animals but about the consequences, politically as so many have noted, of constructions of humanity that deny kinship or shared being with animals. If Elizabeth Costello encounters almost insuperable difficulties in making her case, *Disgrace* offers another possibility:

> Coetzee demonstrates that it is possible for someone once indifferent to animals to become a full-fledged animal lover. For that is the emotion with which David finally approaches the dogs he puts down. In the refuge, he has learned "to concentrate all his attention on the animal they are killing, giving it what he no longer has difficulty in calling by its proper name: love" (219). It is this intense and visceral interaction with animals in the flesh that brought David this revelation. Perhaps if Lucy had, like Elizabeth [Costello], tried to challenge her father intellectually, he would have dismissed her as a crazy animal [advocate]. Instead, David learned through examples set by the animals themselves. Although Coetzee's treatment of the intellectual animal lover [is bleak], his depiction of an intellectual turned animal lover offers hope.[13]

Marianne DeKoven's question, "Why Animals Now?" in the 2009 special issue of *PMLA* indicates the depth of academic interest, to which Coetzee's work has been fundamental. Colleagues like Eric Santner,[14] Julia Reinhard Lupton,[15] and Colleen Boggs theorize creatureliness and animality.[16] A Levinasian ethico-religious frame begins to be invoked for reading Coetzee's work, as, for example, in Alyda Faber, "The Post-Secular Poetics and Ethics of Exposure in J. M. Coetzee's *Disgrace*."[17] To me, all these developments come out of left field, not prefigured by anything I recognize in the old or new South Africa, let alone in the apartheid novel. The developments do, however, give another sense to the term "post-apartheid novel," which does not, in fact, have to represent the situation in post-apartheid South Africa.

It is now fifteen years since *Disgrace* was published. There is no need for me to expatiate on its global impact or on the vast accumulation of critical studies that now adhere to it. The MLA volume, *Approaches to Teaching "Disgrace,"* attests sufficiently to its place in global, Anglophone curricula. I, too, have taught *Disgrace* on occasion in courses on English writing from Southern Africa, beginning with Schreiner's *The Story of an African Farm*. I was initially uncertain about how *Disgrace* would be received by American undergraduates in ethnically mixed but dominantly white classes. I imagined that the narrative context would be strange to them, the novel uncomfortable and potentially depressing, and the aging male protagonist not, in the idiom of the students, "relatable." Not a fun book. Yet, to my surprise, every time I have taught the novel the students have unanimously voted it their favorite among the books they have read in the class. The point of access has tended to be Lurie's "not quite" rape of Melanie, an issue in which feminists and/or women students have a vital stake, but the book presents a wide range of "issues" that spark discussion. I believe the students could and did appreciate the quality of the writing and, despite almost universal hostility to the protagonist, become invested in his consciousness and predicament. I also believe the students had a sense of being called upon to rise to an occasion. All this was so, despite the counter-attractions of the new media, the entertainment industry, and "post-literate" consumer culture.

The surprising receptivity of these students to what I would have considered largely foreign to them has prompted me to reflect on the larger phenomenon of global receptivity to Coetzee's fiction. Those like Imraan Coovadia who have objected to the theoretical cast of Coetzee's mind and writing may, in fact, be missing the point. They tend to treat theory as a reified thing apart, whereas in fact, from the 1970s onward, the language(s) of theory increasingly pervaded literate culture worldwide, becoming, in effect, the language(s)—the cognitive matrix—of our time. Insofar as Coetzee spoke theory, he spoke "our" language, thereby enabling his fiction to hit the spot for so many readers.[18] That is obviously not the only explanation of his pre-eminence, but it is an explanation that suggests why attacks on Coetzee's writing, especially from an anti-theoretical standpoint, have been unable to stop the juggernaut. His fiction has spoken to, and spoken for, his readers, not excluding, I believe, my own undergraduates. Having merely undertaken to discuss J.M. Coetzee "in South Africa," however, I feel that I have now reached the limit of my warrant.

NOTES

1. The name of Lurie's daughter, Lucy, is presumably Wordsworthian, as is her pastoral existence.
2. Notably, Zakes Mda, *Heart of Redness* (London: Picador, 2003); *Ways of Dying* (London: Picador, 2002).
3. Athol Fugard, "I don't want to live in the past," *The Sunday Independent*, Jan. 15, 2001: http://www.lol.co.za/general/newsview.
4. Commentary on this phenomenon by human rights groups and others has been widely reported in the press. See, for example, *Daily Telegraph*, http://www.telegraph.co.uk/news/worldnews/africaandindianocean/southafrica/4982520/Lesbians-subjected-to-corrective-rape-in-South-Africa.html; http://www.cnn.com/2011/WORLD/africa/05/05/south.africa.gay.activist.killed/index.html?hpt=T2.
5. For the record, the TRC was set up in terms of the "Promotion of National Unity and Reconciliation Act, No. 34 of 1995", and was based in Cape Town. The hearings started in 1996. The mandate of the commission was to bear witness to, record and in some cases grant amnesty to the perpetrators of crimes relating to human rights violations, as well as reparation and rehabilitation. Chaired by Archbishop Desmond Tutu, the TRC was considered a model for such tribunals, although its proceedings and results have not been uncontentious. Coetzee's representation of the inquiry into David Lurie's conduct has sometimes been read as a critique of the TRC.
6. Coetzee's brother David, who features in *Boyhood* and died in 2010, was a close friend of my brother Adrian. I never met David, who worked mainly in London as a political activist and journalist.
7. See, for example, Julia Reinhard Lupton, *Afterlives of the Saints: Hagiography, Typology, and Renaissance Literature* (Stanford: Stanford University Press, 1996).
8. For a rich commentary on this episode that keys it to the Homeric contexts invoked in *Disgrace*, see Lars Engle, "*Disgrace* as Uncanny Revision of Gordimer's *None to Accompany Me*," *J.M. Coetzee's Austerities*, Graham Bradshaw and Michael Neill ed. (London: Ashgate, 2010), 107-25. More generally, this chapter offers illuminating commentary on the two books as "post-Apartheid fiction."
9. J.M. Coetzee, *Foe* (New York: Penguin, 1988).
10. Olive Schreiner, *The Story of an African Farm* (New York: Oxford University Press, 1993), 1.
11. That question clearly underlies the land-confiscation—or repossession—in Zimbabwe that became so notorious through the world media, but the politics of land-ownership and redistribution remain a "new" politics of post-apartheid South Africa as well, recently espoused by the EFF leader Julius Malema. Legal land-ownership by whites merely legitimizes historic dispossession and theft, yet the undoing of that ownership poses thorny political and economic problems.
12. In this connection, see Adriaan van Heerden, "Disgrace, Desire, and the Dark Side of the New South Africa," *J.M. Coetzee and Ethics*, 43-64.
13. My thanks to my Dartmouth student Vivien Rendleman for this decisive conclusion.
14. E. L. Santner, *On Creaturely Life: Rilke, Benjamin, Sebald* (Chicago: University of Chicago Press, 2006).
15. Julia Reinhard Lupton, "Creature Caliban," *Shakespeare Quarterly* 51, 1 (200), 1-23.
16. Colleen Glenney Boggs, *Animalia Americana: Animal Representations and Biopolitical Subjectivity* (New York: Columbia University Press, 2013).
17. Faber, "Post-Secular Poetics," *Literature and Theology*, 23, 3 (2009), 303-16
18. I am struck by the breakthrough to international eminence of the South African visual artist William Kentridge, a phenomenon comparable to that of Coetzee's ascent. Kentridge's life-story differs in many salient aspects from Coetzee's, but his work shares a capacity to "leverage" South African tropes into global ones. Something similar applies to the work of the painter Marlene Dumas. This kind of artistic breakout into global eminence and visibility was foreign to the South Africa in which I grew up; no doubt it attests to the now "globalized"

conditions of dissemination and marketing that attenuate distinctions between center and periphery, metropole and provinces.

Chapter Six

Master Classes: *White Writing*

White Writing was published in 1988. By that time, I had settled in the United States, completed a Ph.D. and been a member of the Johns Hopkins English Department for six years. I was in a far better position to understand what Coetzee was doing in his volume devoted to South African writers than I would have been when I first met him. I have already mentioned the Leavisite framework of my undergraduate education and first university teaching experiences, Here, I will add only that in a still-Anglocentric South African critical milieu, a mystique of the gifted amateur critic still held its ground. More was expected of talent, insight, and inspiration than of sustained application and intellectual discipline. Doctoral degrees were viewed with suspicion, while the terminal M.A., with which many Oxbridge students graduated, sufficed as—or was even favored as—a university teaching credential. "Literary criticism"— not, for example, literary scholarship—defined the field of expertise and intellectual activity. It did so not just by default, but powered by a certain militancy.

Gracefulness in writing, even if seldom attained, carried a premium, and the *sprezzatura* commanded by great English critics like Matthew Arnold and William Empson retained a fatal allure, as it may still do to some degree in England. None of this provided a formula for critical productivity. Moreover, superior linguistic proficiency was assumed almost as a birthright, without any need to acquire proficiency in linguistic and grammatical analysis (see *White Writing*. Ch. 5, for the critical payoff from those disciplines).

Elementary composition teaching in Cape Town in 1972 largely consisted of lessons in the recognition and elimination of lower-class markers. Admittedly, that was an extreme for which a particular senior faculty member was responsible, but, still, I discovered when I had to teach undergraduate composition at Berkeley that I first had to teach myself. The cult of the amateur made it extremely difficult to accept professional discipline and forget about airs and graces. The lesson of businesslike professionalism was one Coetzee taught by example more than precept.

That no-nonsense professionalism characterized *White Writing* as well. The protocols of the Americanized academy were fully implemented there. The well-researched essays were models of critical lucidity, force, originality, and purposefulness. If they departed from the professional business as usual, it was by virtue of their ambitious reframing of writing in South Africa, an activity parallel for Coetzee to that of writing fiction in and from South Africa. Coetzee was at the same time teaching his readers lessons, not without a flavor of pedantic didacticism characteristic of his critical writing. If it was necessary or possible for him to *teach* his readership in *White Writing*, it was partly because, although respectable, the critical corpus regarding "South African literature" remained unambitious, provincial, and analytically undeveloped. It is telling that Coetzee had to include so few South African critics in the bibliography to *White Writing*. That would not be the case now.

What might have been inchoate for Coetzee, or merely intuited by him, in the early 1970s could be spelled out definitively in 1988. That went not just for Coetzee's ambitious remapping of the South African writing scene in *White Writing*, but also for the nature of critical reading in our time:

> Our ears today are finely attuned to the modes of silence. We have been brought up on the music of Webern : substantial silence structured by tracings of sound. Our craft is all in reading *the other*: gaps, inverses, undersides; the veiled, the dark, the feminine, alterities . . . only part of the truth, such reading asserts, resides in what writing says of the hitherto unsaid; for the rest, its truth lies in what it dare not say for its own safety, or in what it does not know about itself; in its silences. It is a mode of reading which subverts the dominant, [but] is in peril, like all triumphant subversion, of becoming the dominant in turn (81).

In 1988, this seemed like a decisive clarification, and it still has something of that force. It was especially pertinent to the discussion of the South African *plaasroman*, with its palpable silence regarding the presence of black people as the labor force on South African farms. It was their "absence" that needed to be read in the *plaasroman*. In principle, what Coetzee adumbrated about reading in general had to apply to the reading of his own works; I have tried to apply the lesson in practice as occasion has required in this chapter. Coetzee added suggestively that a wish to restore open, explicit, self-sufficient meanings was itself a pastoral fantasy, ultimately that of the edenic language.

Much of *White Writing* that now seems familiar enough to attract no attention was still being consolidated during the 1980s. That includes the book's multilingual interdisciplinarity, a far cry from the "English" literary criticism of yore. Unusually, the book considers writings in English and Afrikaans side by side, as well as identifying some essentially colonial preoccupations that cross the boundary between them.[1] The book's subtitle, "The Culture of Letters in South Africa," signified the continuing displacement of "literature" by "culture" as the principal object of inquiry and frame of reference in critical studies. In *White Writing*, the non-judgmental stance of the student of culture enabled Coetzee to include English poets, for example, who would previously have been dismissed as merely "bad." The chapter entitled "The Picturesque, the Sublime, and the South African Landscape" capitalized on recent developments in the study of Romanticism and the sublime in both European and American literature and painting, although of course the trick here was to triangulate the configuration by making South Africa one of its points. In short, *White Writing* was a book that bore the strong imprint of its moment. It brought the world home to South Africa, and moved a "new" South Africa into the world, as Coetzee's fiction had already done.

Specifically as contribution to the interpretation of South African texts, *White Writing* began by defining its field, not as that of South African literature, but of white writing, a Coetzee coinage: ". . .the phrase *white writing* does [not] imply the existence of a body of literature different in nature from black writing. White writing is white only insofar as it is generated by the concerns of people no longer European, not yet African" (11).[2] It is, in other words, a transitional or interstitial phenomenon, permanently "rooted" neither in Europe nor Africa. That definition solved a longstanding problem in which South African literature was expected either to ratify or to manifest South African identity, a "highly problematical" (8) expectation, to say the least (my earlier pages should have suggested just how problematical.)[3] Coetzee returns often to the topic of how writers in English and Afrikaans tried to make their writing more African or South African, but that is a different matter from suggesting that their writing manifests any essentially South African identity.

Coetzee makes it clear that *White Writing* is not a literary history but an essay collection. He makes no attempt at "coverage;" indeed, he mentions only in passing writers of the stature of Nadine Gordimer and Doris Lessing, and, among poets, Roy Campbell. Despite the magisterial authority projected by the book, it is still possible for readers to suspect a certain willful idiosyncrasy in Coetzee's choices: Early ethnography of the Hottentots? Sarah Gertrude Millin? Thomas Pringle? C.M. Van Den Heever? In what follows, I will try to make sense (perhaps no more than my own sense) of these and other choices, both separately and collectively. That will entail my asking what investments on Coetzee's part in South Africa the book represents. I will simply call these investments circumstantial rather than try to get further behind them in, for example, psychoanalytic or ideological terms.

If there is one thing that characterizes Coetzee's criticism in *White Writing*, it is his unusually respectful, patient, engagement with writers and topics that would normally have been bypassed or curtly dismissed in the criticism of 1988. These include the farm novels of the Afrikaans novelist C. M. van den Heever, whom few Anglo-South Africans would ever have read, and whose "Afrikaans idea," as he called it, would typically have been dismissed as "Afrikaner ideology." The last days of apartheid would not necessarily have seemed like a propitious time to engage with the "boer" idyll of the family farm. Coetzee could not have been more aware of that fact, but, as all his South African fiction indicates, he was himself sufficiently invested in that idyll to give serious attention to Van Den Heever and to the English writer Pauline Smith. In the case of Van Den Heever especially, that meant engaging with tropes of organic rootedness deriving proximately from the German *Bauerroman* (tainted by Nazism) and ultimately from European Romanticism, in which Coetzee was also heavily invested. (Indeed, his protagonist Lurie in *Disgrace* seems like the Last Romantic in South Africa.) These were, in a sense, risky investments even when subjected to the most rigorous critique.

Living dangerously also meant engaging with the 1920s novelist Sarah Gertrude Millin, practically forgotten by the 1980s or else repudiated on account of her own investment in the ideology of racial purity and corresponding stigmatization of hybrid "degeneracy." Coetzee emphasizes that Millin was both Jewish and a vehement critic of Nazism, but she continued to regard racial intermarriage as a taint that could never be expunged from the bloodline. Such is her "tragedy of blood," of which, ironically, her own work now carries the taint.

In the cases of both Van Den Heever and Millin, the "lessons" Coetzee was teaching connected those now-suspect writers to earlier, dominant forms of thought in Europe, thereby enabling properly informed, non-trivializing, readings of their work. By implication, such readings were generally lacking in in South African criticism. *White Writing* raised the bar. Coetzee was also, however, introducing these writers to an international readership, a challenge that few if any had ever considered taking up. That meant presenting these writers, and others in the book, not as outlying "South African writers" practically below the threshold of visibility, but rather as white writers under Coetzee's definition, participating both intelligibly and interestingly, for better or worse, in an intellectual culture shared by the global readership, by no means all ethnically "white," to which *White Writing* is addressed.

The novels of C.M van den Heever become Coetzee's principal case in point. Van den Heever, in Coetzee's estimation, the "most considerable" writer of farm novels in Afrikaans, takes a specific feature of Afrikaner farm inheritance as his fictional starting point. Customarily, the farm would be divided at the death of the father and shared between the sons. Once unlimited land was no longer available from further "trekking" into the interior, farms were divided into increasingly uneconomical units. That was the problem solved under English law by primogeniture. Primogeniture obviously has its own problems, as evidenced by Shakespeare's *As You Like It* and *King Lear*, but equitable Afrikaner inheritance of South African farmland made individual farming increasingly unsustainable, and also opened the door to competition and conniving between widows and sons, between sons and intrusive blood-relations, and between those who sought to hold the land and those willing to sell or alienate it. The vulnerability of farms to drought, market fluctuations, and other adverse circumstances made them insecure, and the mortgaging of farms frequently meant their loss to those with the means to purchase them or fund their purchase: in *plaasroman* demonology, Jews, bankers, and other urban monied interests.

Conflict and conniving supply much of the drama of Van den Heever's farm novels, but what is of primary concern to Van den Heever in Coetzee's account is the Afrikaner order and values threatened by such conflict:

> In the myth of natural right elaborated by Van den Heever, the founding fathers pay for the farm in blood, sweat, and tears, not in money; they hack it out of the primeval bush, they defend it against barbarians, they leave their bones behind in the soil. Inherited ownership of the farm thus becomes a sacred trust; to alienate the farm means to forsake the bones of the ancestors . . . natural right must be reestablished in each generation by good stewardship of the ancestral estate (85).

> We must note that into the myth of the good marriage of the farmer to his farm are drawn many of the energies of European Romanticism, many of the feelings of cosmic identification and engulfment originally attributed not to the relation of the farmer and his farm but of man to the wilderness, to forest and moor and mountain (87).

Within this framework, plenitude of being derives from self-assimilation within the inheriting lineage—along with the forefathers and descendants— rather than from isolated individuality. The assumption of trans-individual identity becomes virtually a moment of rebirth and awakening into a new mode of non-reflective consciousness, accompanied by a new capacity to "read" the land. The plight of the individual, on the other hand, is that of debilitation and melancholia about the transience of things. That *weemoed* can be overcome only by assuming transpersonal identity: "Never before had he felt such a bond with the earth. It was now as if the life within it were streaming into his body" (86). The real drama of Van den Heever's novels, according to Coetzee, is that of epiphany, when the Afrikaner farmer comes to consciousness as a member of the lineage, at one with the land, rather than as an individual. Coetzee adds: "Van den Heever writes about the spiritual self-realization of few in South Africa save the Afrikaner" (87) (and, what is more, Afrikaners enjoying the privileged dispensation of land-ownership).

Perhaps unexpectedly, some characters in the novels, notably in *Laat Vrugte (Late Fruit)*, resist assimilation into the transpersonal dimension of the lineage, or, if they are women, have no access to it. Women may indeed feel enslaved or suffocated by the ancestral will, while even men like the protagonist Sybrand may become aware of the ancestors as unwanted domestic intruders. Worse still, for the individualistic Sybrand, the ancestors batten on the living like needy ghosts, vicariously reliving their own failed lives through their descendants and eventually summoning them to death. Coetzee avers that *Laat Vrugte* is not simply a story of the haunted farm, nor does it mark a turnabout on Van den Heever's part. The novel's hauntology attests at most to the ambiguity of the "dark forces" with which protagonists in the *plaasroman*, like some in D.H. Lawrence's fiction, want to get in touch; it is more like a negative confirmation than a refutation of Van den Heever's myth-making.

Such, then, is Van den Heever's "idea of the Afrikaner." For obvious reasons, it is not an idea that ever recommended itself to Anglo-South Africans, to say the least, or to anyone else, yet it is a recognizable instantiation of an "idea" that, for better or worse—mostly for worse?—has had an important European and American history. While recognizing Van den Heever's failures and limitations, Coetzee does justice, as no one writing in English or Afrikaans had done, to the energy and weightiness of his novels, as well as to their accomplished "transfer" of a Romantic epistemology into South African white writing. Coetzee's ability to inhabit Van den Heever's writing position is characteristic of all his critical dealings with writers who interest him. Sometimes the inhabiting seems quite personal here, as when he writes of a Van den Heever character "without a farm to inherit, it is unclear what social role he can play but that of teacher and yearner after farm life" (93).

If Van den Heever's Afrikaans-language novels were practically unknown to English-language readers, something similar applied, at least in 1988, to the writings of late nineteenth and early twentieth century English-language poets like Thomas Pringle and H.H. Dugmore. Even as a South African academic, I had never felt obliged to read these poets; their work could easily be bypassed as mere verse, of historical interest at best. Coetzee connects these poets to what proves to be a rich topic in *White Writing*, namely the (mostly failing) effort by poets writing in English and Afrikaans to fill the "empty" space of Africa and render the harsh, alien landscape tractable to poetic inscription. The equipment Pringle brought with him, namely the rhetorical and painterly machinery of the European sublime and picturesque, did not necessarily "transfer" to the South African landscape. European landscape painting cherished lush vegetation, still or moving water, light and shade, all lacking in the landscapes Pringle wished to render. Flatness, endlessness, and uniform brightness did not compose themselves into a "prospect" viewed from above. Complaints about the deficiencies of the landscape began to be heard; these persisted in the work of later English-language poets. Coetzee contrasts the failed transfer of both the sublime and the picturesque to South Africa with their relatively successful transfer to America, Luminist painting being a case in point. If the difference lies partly in the American landscape, with its grand, natural vistas, it lies as well in the correspondingly grand imperial vistas that increasingly possessed the American imagination. As in the case of Van den Heever, Coetzee's backtracking from South Africa into Romanticism provides the needed framework of intelligibility.

The book's opening chapter, "Idleness in South Africa," might be said to reveal a risky investment of a different kind. In *Boyhood* and *Summertime*, Coetzee declares an interest in the languages and peoples that antedated Dutch settlement in the Western Cape. It is with those that the boy feels an affinity, partly because they are actually or virtually extinct. The people in question are the so-called Bushmen and Hottentots, these names now being, or having become, derogatory. Yet the preferred anthropological usage, San (Bushmen) and Khoikoin (Hottentots), has its own problems. The term San was already applied as a derogatory one by the Khoikoi. Many, including some of the people in question, have reverted to "Bushmen." "Hottentot," on the other hand, is now offensive, partly on account of its debasement into "hotnot," an insulting Afrikaans term for any mixed-race person. Yet avoiding offense comes at the price of a certain stilted correctness when San and Khoisan are used in non-technical English; they are also general categories for people who might prefer to identify themselves tribally. In any event, when Coetzee uses the term Hottentot in his chapter, it is in deference to the usage of eighteenth and nineteenth century ethnographers and travel writers.

The effect of encountering "Idleness in South Africa" as the first chapter of *White Writing* (it had previously been published in in 1980 in *English Studies in Africa*, 23, 1 [1980]) was mildly perplexing and disorienting. "Idleness" seemed eccentric both as a critical and an anthropological topic: what did the term mean, what was there to say about it, and why did it matter? Next, the chapter dealt primarily with the journals of European travelers to South Africa, and did not therefore qualify as "white writing" under Coetzee's definition. Third, the chapter's focus on Hottentots was a departure from the dominantly black-white schema of apartheid era writing. That could have been seen as diversionary in the era of anti-apartheid struggle. Historical and anthropological inquiry had by no means bypassed the

Khokoin, but they no longer existed as a separate entity in the political reckoning of the 1980s; their descendants had largely been swept into the apartheid basket as Colored.[4] The remnants of the Bushmen had, on the other hand, been exiled to arid, remote areas of South Africa and Namibia.[5]

Perhaps Coetzee was giving further evidence of a subjective investment and making a point about what was mostly excluded from current view: both this people's history and extensive travel-archives of the eighteenth and nineteenth centuries. The boy-protagonist of *Boyhood* further evinces an interest in what might be called the autochthonous peoples of the Western Cape, a category that includes neither whites nor blacks. In the eyes of the boy-protagonist, they alone are ontologically grounded, so to speak, in the Cape, and in them alone can traces of an original ethnic purity be discerned. This boy's view is not that of the adult writer—uncorrupted racial "purity" belongs to the discredited Sarah Gertrude Millin—but it remains somewhat provocatively in play in *Boyhood,* pre-empting both white and black proprietary claims to the Western Cape. Moreover, by writing so extensively about the Hottentots, Coetzee departs from the prevailing, codified "racial" discourse of South Africa.

In addition to that, Coetzee's mining of the travel writings confronts us with more otherness than we are accustomed to processing. One travel writer after another comments on the Hottentots' inability to conceive of a god, on their unregulated promiscuity in shared living quarters, on their custom of smearing their entire bodies with animal excrement, on their habit of devouring whole animal carcasses including unwashed entrails, on the filth and stink of their dwelling places, and, above all, on their idleness. They refuse to make more than the minimum effort needed to sustain themselves by hunting and gathering, and evince no interest in improving their quality of life by saving or laboring. They strongly resist white efforts to force them to work. Both the elementariness of Hottentot life and the phenomenon of their idleness—the latter especially—become an unfathomable scandal to Europeans by now fully conditioned to the "Protestant work ethic." Forgetting the brutal subjugation required to reduce pre-modern Europeans to the discipline of labor, writers and preachers are at once outraged and baffled by Hottentot idleness; it became the task of Moravian missionaries to discipline and "socialize" the Hottentots. Moreover, if the Hottentots represented too much difference, they also paradoxically failed to represent enough: like other colonial natives, they were also acknowledged to be human. On both counts, they failed to feed the increasingly voracious, standardized machinery of eighteenth and nineteenth century comparative ethnography. In other words, they threatened to be unwritable within that framework, and thus escape the cognitive net.

Indeed, the Hottentots presented *no* threat in the military sense or by virtue of having a conflicting advanced culture; the threat they represented was that of maintaining an "idleness" radically at odds with the European imperial mission and utterly heterogeneous to the Protestant, European norm of industriousness and providence. Not a single European writer entertains the thought that the Hottentots incarnate the ancient pastoral ideal of otium, a carefree, chosen indolence. Nor do they pose the question whether the Hottentots have more to lose than to gain by enslaving themselves to farm labor on others' behalf.

What intensifies the threat of Hottentot idleness is that it can seemingly communicate itself to the burghers of the Cape, denounced, in turn, for their regression to idleness and sloth. According to Coetzee, that propensity remains actively threatening even after 1948, when anti-miscegenation laws prevent whites, Afrikaners above all, from "idly" cohabiting with the native population and producing large, unregulated families.

From a literary perspective, this chapter conceives of South Africa as the site of a lost, "low" utopianism exemplified by Hottentot life. Although that utopianism is outlawed by every legal and rhetorical means, it remains visible in the travel writings of European visitors to the Cape. By invoking both an ethnographic perspective and an archive of travel writings, Coetzee aligned the critical discourse of South Africa with prevailing trends of the same kind in early modern and American studies preoccupied with new world expansion and colonial encounters. Significantly, Coetzee begins with Jodocus Hondius's *A Clear Description of the Cape of Good Hope* (1727), thus shifting backwards the temporal horizon of white writing in South Africa.[6] From the perspective of whites, the Hottentot utopia could be conceived only in negative terms. More often than not, South African peoples and landscapes seem to have presented themselves to those seeking to "master" them as frustrating negatives and negations.

In addition to noting the large-scale erasure of black people in white writing, whether the *plaasroman* or poetic confrontations with an "empty" land, Coetzee also discusses the representation of a colored man, Tooings ("Tatters") in an eponymous series of novels by the 1930s Afrikaans author H.H. Kuhn, writing under the pen-name of Mikro. Even in Coetzee's paraphrase, these novels make for painful and embarrassing reading. As it pertains to himself, Tooings has internalized the racist discourse of the patriarchal white farmer, valorized in the novels. Tooings perceives himself as "rubbish," undeserving of respect, and as entitled to no other name than the demeaning one assigned by his paternalistic employer. His recurrent impulse to revolt invariably dies out in a grateful return to the paternal fold. These books are less a representation of a person of color than an image of the mental and social world of its Afrikaner readers during the 1930s. That possibility always exists when persons of color appear in white writing.

Coetzee takes on Alan Paton in the chapter "Simple Language, Simple People: Smith, Paton, Mikro" (11 5–35). As author of *Cry, the Beloved*

Country (1948), Paton was probably the "white writer" from South Africa who enjoyed more worldwide recognition than any other; to this day, he tends to be the one popularly associated with South African fiction. Film versions of the novel have extended its reach. As the quintessential white, liberal, novel of conscience emanating from the world of apartheid, *Cry, the Beloved Country* took on a sanctified status in and out of South Africa, and, in effect, launched the white-writing genre of the anti-apartheid novel. Paton's public role as leader of the non-racial South African Liberal Party combined with his authorship to make him the iconic white South African liberal of his time.

Of all this, Coetzee would have been well aware, just as he would probably have been aware that Paton was a complex, contradictory figure, whose authoritarian personality did no always endear him. A protégé of J.H. Hofmeyr, South Africa's World War II deputy prime minister—*de facto* prime minister in Smuts's frequent absences—Paton shared Hofmeyr's evangelically-tinged Anglicanism, and participated with Hofmeyr in outdoor Christian boys'-club activities.[7] Hofmeyr's liberalism, like Paton's, was strongly conditioned by religious language and conviction, the presence of which in *Cry, the Beloved Country* allowed many to feel moved—Paton could do that—and conscience-stricken, but also reassured that they were not being summoned to revolution.

Given Paton's eminence, Coetzee appears to give him short shrift in *White Writing*. He brackets Paton with Mikro (Mikro!) and Pauline Smith in a single chapter. "Debunking" is too strong a word, yet Coetzee evinces less sympathy with Paton than he does with other writers with less impeccable liberal credentials. In his fully justified critique of Paton's faux-Zulu, he nevertheless overlooks the fact that Paton was sometimes reproducing Khumalo's literal English translations of isi-Zulu locutions and words, for example "heavy" for *sinda*, where the term refers to an enormous burden of sadness and emotional distress.

Khumalo is an impoverished, rural Anglican clergyman low down in the hierarchy, and the novel concerns his efforts on behalf of his son, who has committed a murder in Johannesburg, for which he is eventually executed. The language of Paton's "translation" is strongly inflected by the seventeenth century English of the Authorized Version; in Paton's rendering, it is a language of archaic, stately nobility inhospitable to lying. For that reason, Khumalo's brother, the Johannesburg politician and demagogue, prefers to speak in English. English is also more urbane than the vernacular. Paton channels his profound distrust of black politics as distinct from black spiritual uplift through the representation of the brother, Khumalo's corrupt alter ego.

En route by train to Johannesburg, other passengers have to induct Khumalo into the nature of urban life in the goldfields. That induction includes an explanation of gold mining. Having to explain it in "simple English" produces a satirical defamiliarizing effect, yet it is also necessary for his informants to explain things to Khumalo in an archaic language seemingly without a technical vocabulary or modern coordinates. Examples Coetzee cites include "fire-sticks" (dynamite), "chimney" (mine-shaft) and "go away" (run for cover). Coetzee points out that isi-Zulu possesses the word *udalimede* for dynamite, *umgodi* (hole in the earth) for shaft ("chimney" is *ushimela*), and *banda* for take cover. Moreover, in the passage Coetzee cites (127), it would appear that the Zulu language cannot encompass large numbers: "it goes up in a cage, up a long chimney, so long that I cannot say it for you." The ceremonious repetition that characterizes polite exchanges between "Zulu" speakers, like Khumalo and his wife, in *Cry, the Beloved Country* belong to a world in which time is clearly not of the essence. Paton's translations, or "transfers" as Coetzee calls them, invest isi-Zulu with a static, pre-technological character threatened by industrial modernity, yet in fact isi-Zulu is no exception to the rule that living languages borrow or coin the terms they need in changing circumstances: *udalimede* and *ushimela* are clearly derived from English words that have been incorporated into, and naturalized in, isi-Zulu. Paton's "Zulu" poignantly belongs, in fact, to an imaginary better world, with Old Testament overtones, now on the verge of disappearance. "Khumalo's aspiration, in the wake of his son's death, is to hold together the remnants of his community in a muted version of black pastoral" (*White Writing*, 129). Yet while approving Khumalo's stoic nobility, Paton sees the writing on the wall. Coetzee acknowledges that Paton gives the last word in the novel to the young, black, agricultural officer, who knows Khumalo's world is gone: it is an old man's dream, dispelled by contemporary economics and demographics. The young man is polite and respectful, but he is a young professional who happens to be Zulu, representing the novel's best possible future—educated, technological, apolitical—rather than the past.

In Coetzee's own writing, the best test case for the representation of a person of color and his language is probably that of Petrus in *Disgrace*. If the direct speech in English attributed to him is simple almost to the point of being monosyllabic, it does not follow that he is a simple person or that his speech constitutes a translation of a simpler language than English. He can "savor" the inflections of the English phrase "dog-man," his initial title on Lucy's farm (64). Although his English is subtly marked as non-standard through inversions, repetitions, and faintly unidiomatic locutions, it is not defective. He is also technologically competent, more so than Lurie, and knows how to work the modern financial system. Insofar as Lurie seems to yield to the simplifying impulse, it is in framing Petrus as a "peasant"—but then, so is Ettinger in his eyes—and the "peasant" he has in mind is the ambitious, conniving peasant-farmer with a European lineage. Deviousness and malice are part of that stereotype, and Lurie's suspicion, dislike, and anger mount after the event of the rape, during which Petrus has been mysteriously absent from the farm. For all Lurie's imaginative projection, however, conditioned by his historical and literary consciousness, Petrus remains impenetrable (as does Lucy, for that matter), largely by failing to respond to the demands and questions of Lurie as an unentitled interrogator. He generally chooses not to take Lurie's questions as questions, responding at a tangent. Practically every utterance leaves more palpably unsaid than said, at least to the frustrated Lurie. Ultimately, there is precisely no way Lurie and, *a fortiori*, the novel can get "inside" Petrus as a subject, and that is precisely the incapacity that marks the limits of Lurie's cultural formation and interpretive repertoire. What goes for Lurie goes for the novel, since Petrus, like practically everything in *Disgrace*, is mediated by Lurie's consciousness. Thus Coetzee dodges the bullet of "simple language, simple people," yet only at the cost of a certain frustration on the part of the reader. That frustration may simply bring back the complaint that Coetzee cannot or will not empathetically represent the subjectivity of a black person. Alternatively, it may be the salutary frustration experienced upon arrival at a scrupulously staged impasse, with significant political and cultural implications.[8] It is a lesson in white writing.

It is not clear that the era of white writing as Coetzee defined it is over in South Africa or anywhere else, at least in the postcolonial zone. To that extent, *White Writing* retains its currency. But is Coetzee himself still a white writer? Recent, talented Afrikaans women writers like Dalene Matthee, Marlene van Niekerk and Ingrid Winterbach are not necessarily white writers in Coetzee's sense. Nor, obviously, are writers of color like Njabulo Ndebele, Zoe Wicomb, Zakes Mda, or Kopano Matlwa. Some, like Peter Abrahams, Richard Rive, Alex la Guma, and Bessie Head never were, although, insofar as they wrote in English, they did not write wholly outside English conventions. The now substantial body of Coetzee's criticism and reviewing is not, however, wholly focused on white writing and its issues. He has ranged widely over writers whose provenance varies considerably. Yet what remains consistent across this range is Coetzee's relentless preoccupation with the formal challenges and problems of *writing*. He belongs to a moment in which writing took a sharply self-reflexive turn, as everyone recognizes, but none in our time have applied themselves as rigorously, continuously, and responsibly to realizing the consequences of that turn as Coetzee has. That does not make him the "formalist" some have charged him with being; as we have seen, he is very far from lacking interest, in either sense of the word, in the historical and material particulars of South African life. For him, however, the question is always what raises particulars to the level of significance. For him, there is never a short cut that bypasses conscious, formal representation.

NOTES

1. Coetzee obviously could not consider black vernacular writing under the title "white writing," nor did he have the linguistic equipment to do so. He does, however, mention the black poet H.I.E. Dhlomo (174), whose poetic diction in English is that of white pastoral.

2. Throughout this chapter, I have taken the term "white writing" simply in the way Coetzee defines and uses it. In other words, I have not pursued the conceit of "white writing" as invisible writing, or self-cancelling-writing. Coetzee may or may not have known that the term had a history in French feminist theorizing of *écriture féminine*. There, the term embodied the conceit of writing in breast milk rather than ink. I see no connection between this use of the term and Coetzee's.

3. The South African poet Roy Campbell, for example, known as "Zulu" to prewar Bloomsbury (where he was by no means universally well received), attempted in his poems and autobiographical writings to project a hypermasculine "colonial" persona distinct from those of his homophobically reviled English male contemporaries. For him, hyperbolic self-fabrication rather than mere self-fashioning could fill the "empty" space of Africa and connect the colonial subject to primordial "African" vitality. South African social life and literary culture presented themselves to him, in contrast, as a spectacle of farcical mediocrity, to be chastised in satirical verse. In later life Campbell became a Catholic expatriate living in Spain, supporting the cause of Franco, and indulging in supposedly Mithraic equestrian mysticism.

4. Some Griquas have now reclaimed the Khoisan name and nationality, furthermore accusing the ANC of cultural genocide in still classifying them along with Coloreds and refusing to negotiate with them or other First Nations. See, for example, *Space van Adriana: Boer Genocide in South Africa*, https://nolstuijt.wordpress.com/ category/indigenous-first-nations-khoi-san-griqua-south-africa/. Nomenclature remains tricky in this field. The case of Saartjie Baartman (1790–1815), the so-called Hottentot Venus, who was treated as a freak-show exhibit in England and whose remains were preserved as medical specimens in Paris after her death, has received a great deal of attention in feminist/anti-racist writing. In the US, however, she has been quite widely assimilated as the generic Black Woman, whereas she would not have been that in nineteenth century South Africa; she would have been regarded as distinct from black, African women. This is not to deny that both Khoisan and African women were victims of an overarching, sexist, racism. At the request of Nelson Mandela, her remains were repatriated and buried in South Africa in 2002.

5. Where, however, they were rounded up by the South African military during the 1980s for use as trackers, a role they had been induced to play by practically every white military force operating in South Africa since at least 1902.

6. Jodocus Hondius, *A Clear Description of the Cape of Good Hope*, tr. L.C van Oordt (Cape Town: Van Riebeeck Festival Book Exhibition Committee, 1952).

7. Paton himself wrote a biography of Hofmeyr that evokes their world of evangelical enthusiasm. Initially published under the title *Hofmeyr*, it was republished as *South African Tragedy: The Life and Times of Jan Hofmeyr* (New York: Scribner's, 1965).

8. See, in this connection, Gayatri Charavorty Spivak, "Ethics and Politics in Tagore, Coetzee, and Certain Scenes of Teaching," *Diacritics*, Vol. 32, No. 3/4, Ethics (Autumn - Winter, 2002), 17–31. The situation becomes less intractable when a black actor plays the role of Petrus, thus communicating a subjective will and "live" presence. Eriq Ebouaney did so in the 2008 film of *Disgrace* directed by Anna Maria Monticelli. In a remarkable performance, Ebouaney, a French speaker who also played Patrice Lumumba in the eponymous film, captured the accent and inflections of English as spoken by a Xhosa speaker (Ebouaney is not even listed as starring in the Wikipedia entry.) The globalization of film making adds a multicultural "performative" layer to the politics of the novel: a film about South Africa made in Australia by a Moroccan-born director, with the Parisian son of Camerounian immigrants playing a Xhosa character in the Eastern Cape, with an American leading man (John Malkovich), mimicking Coetzee, and with a South African leading lady (Jessica Haines).

www.ingramcontent.com/pod-product-compliance
Lightning Source LLC
Chambersburg PA
CBHW030117010526
44116CB00005B/293